The
Non
Connoisseur's
Menu Guide

Also by David D'Aprix

*International Foreign Language Guide for
Hotel Employees*

The *Non* Connoisseur's Menu Guide

TO ORDERING AND ENJOYING FRENCH, ITALIAN, AND SPANISH/LATIN AMERICAN CUISINE

David D'Aprix

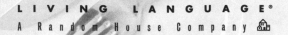

LIVING LANGUAGE®
A Random House Company

Published by Living Language, 201 East 50th Street, New York, New York 10022

Random House, Inc. New York, Toronto, London, Sydney, Auckland

Living Language is a registered trademark of Random House, Inc.

Manufactured in the United States of America

ILLUSTRATIONS BY NICOLE KAUFMAN
DESIGN BY LYNNE AMFT

Library of Congress Cataloging-in-Publication Data
D'Aprix, David.
The non-connoisseur's menu guide/by David D'Aprix.
1. Food Dictionaries—Polyglot. 2. Dictionaries, Polyglot.
I. Title.
TX350.D37   1999
641.3'003—dc21   99-35433
CIP

ISBN 0-609-80493-6

10   9   8   7   6   5   4   3   2   1

First Edition

ACKNOWLEDGMENTS

Many thanks to the Living Language staff: Lisa Alpert, Andrea Rosen, Ana Stojanović, Chris Warnasch, Christopher Medellín, Eric Sommer, Germaine Ma, Helen Tang, Vincent La Scala, Lynne Amft, David Tran, Giuseppe Pezzotti and Leta Evanthes.

CONTENTS

CONTENTS

Italian Menu Guide

CONTENTS

Spanish & Latin American Menu Guide

CONTENTS

The

Non

Connoisseur's

Menu Guide

INTRODUCTION

THE NON-CONNOISSEUR'S MENU GUIDE will heighten your dining experience, and you'll never feel embarrassed again while you guess at the meaning and pronunciation of menu selections. Ever wonder about the origins of *vichyssoise*? Read the "Did you know?" note on page 17, and you might be surprised by what you learn. Still trying to figure out how to pronounce *gnocchi*? Look on page 118, and you'll settle it once and for all. And the Spanish/Latin American section will have you reading *tapas* menus like a pro in no time. So just tuck this book in your pocket and you'll be ready to dine in any restaurant from here to Paris, Rome, or Buenos Aires!

The Non-Connoisseur's Menu Guide is divided by language and cuisine into three sections: French, Italian, and Spanish/Latin American. Each section begins with an introduction to the cuisine of the region and includes a variety of typical dishes, from aperitifs to appetizers to desserts. We have also included an invaluable section on the complexities of ordering wine and coffee. English translations and the pronunciation of each item are also included. A glossary of useful terms such as meats, vegetables, and food preparation makes it easy to look up anything on a menu that has you stumped.

You can use this guide in three ways. First, simply look up the menu item in the appropriate section—appetizer, salad, soup, entrée, etc. If it's not there (because there are thousands of possible menu descriptions, and the guide features a selection of the most common—and some of the more creative—menu items you're likely to find) just turn to the glossary section and find the individual words describing the dish. That way, even if you miss a word or two, you'll have a solid idea of what the menu item is all about. The third way to use this guide is simply to sit back and read it when you have a few spare moments. With a little imagination, you'll find yourself relaxing in a cozy French bistro, people-watching in a busy Italian sidewalk café, or hearing the lively sounds of a mariachi band. There are enough cultural and culinary tips and bits of trivia to occupy your attention as you peruse the vocabulary. You'll also find a few helpful phrases in French, Italian, and Spanish to take you through your meal in style. And with the help of a few words of wisdom from chefs, waiters, and restaurant owners, before you know it you'll be on your way to becoming a culinary expert!

We know *The Non-Connoisseur's Menu Guide* will enhance your dining experiences. The world of food encompassed by French, Italian, Spanish, and Latin American cuisines is vast, and we hope that you'll be inspired to continue to explore this delectable universe!

Bon appétit!

Buon appetito!

¡Buen provecho!

French

MENU GUIDE

Introduction to French Cuisine

WELCOME TO THE WORLD OF FRENCH restaurants! It's impossible to say enough about France's long culinary tradition. Images of romantic, elegant, and sophisticated dining inevitably arise from the mere thought of French food: rich dishes laden with sauces, luscious wines, and extravagant desserts. But that's not all you should expect. The basic tenet of French cooking is fresh food simply prepared. Flavorful stews, roasts, and sautés are accompanied by fresh vegetables and creative potato dishes. From the simplest onion soup to a rich *pâté en croûte* (pah-tay ah^n KROOT), French food is sure to delight you.

GETTING STARTED . . .

Une table pour deux personnes.	*A table for two.*
ewn TAH-bluh pour DUH pehr-SOHN	
La carte, s'il vous plaît.	*The menu, please.*
lah KAHRT seel voo PLEH	
La carte des vins.	*The wine list.*
lah KAHRT day VEH^N	
Je voudrais . . .	*I'd like . . .*
zhuh vood-REH	

Aperitifs

A FRENCH RESTAURANT in the United States will certainly offer the full range of alcoholic beverages. But why not start your meal like the French? Various *apéritifs* (ah-pay-ree-TEEF) are very popular alternatives to the American cocktails. Many are also referred to as "bitters" because they have an initial sweet taste with a slightly bitter aftertaste. They may be either wine- or spirit-based. Wine-based aperitifs are still wines fortified with distilled spirits and are often flavored with herbs and spices. The alcohol content ranges from 16 to 22 percent. Spirit-based aperitifs start with distilled spirits and then add flavorings, and may be much stronger.

Wine is also commonly drunk as an aperitif. Don't ignore champagne, which makes a lovely predinner drink. A *kir* (keer), which is white wine with a touch of *crème de cassis* (krehm duh kah-SEES), black currant liqueur, can be quite festive. Or consider a *kir royale* (keer rwah-YAHL), which is champagne topped with Chambord, a classy raspberry liqueur. So drink up, wet your palate, and whet your appetite! *Videz les verres* (vee-day lay VEHR)! Bottoms up!

Amer Picon (ah-MEHR pee-KOH^N)

A very popular French bitter. Forty percent alcohol. Contains oranges, gentian root, and quinine. Drink it with club soda and a twist of lemon.

Americano (ah-meh-ree-kah-NOH)

A cocktail of two great aperitifs: Campari and vermouth, on the rocks.

Byrrh (BEER)

A blend of red wine and quinine water with a bittersweet aftertaste. Drink with club soda.

Cin-Cin (CHEEN-CHEEN)

Sweet and dry vermouth mixed, served on ice. The name comes from Cinzano, an Italian brand of vermouth.

Dubonnet (dew-boh-NEH), **Rouge** (ROOZH) **or Blanc** (BLAH^N)

Both are 18 percent alcohol, with a semi-sweet taste and a hint of quinine. Serve chilled or on the rocks, with a twist of lemon.

Lillet (lee-LEH)

Made from a blend of wine, brandy, fruits, and herbs. It has a nice fruity, citric, slightly herby taste. Very elegant, delicious with ice and a bit of club soda, and maybe a piece of citrus fruit.

PHRASES FOR ORDERING DRINKS IN FRENCH:

sec	straight
SEHK	
avec des glaçons	on the rocks
ah-VEHK day glah-SOH^N	
à l'eau	with water
ah LOH	

Martini (mahr-tee-NEE)

The standard French way to refer to vermouth. Refers to the brand name, Martini & Rossi. You must specify red or white. If you want one, either order a vermouth or clarify that you don't want the famous gin concoction.

Martini Cocktail (mahr-tee-NEE kohk-TEHL)

The real one! Mostly gin, with a tiny amount of vermouth. There is not, nor ever will be, a better cocktail. It's not French. It's American, our contribution to the world of drinks. It seems to preface all food very well. Remember the rule with martinis: one is not enough, three are too many.

> " *A good aperitif should be like a ringing bell to Pavlov's dog. It should 'open the appetite' and serve almost as an appetizer.*
>
> ROBERT MCELROY
> CHEZ ES SAADA, NEW YORK "

Negroni (neh-groh-NEE)

A blend of gin, sweet vermouth, and Campari served over ice. Be careful.

Pastis (pah-STEES), *Pernod* (pehr-NOH), *Ricard* (ree-KAHR)

Anise-flavored liquor. Pastis is the modern version of the original absinthe, which included wormwood in its formula. Wormwood was outlawed in most of the world in 1915, and in 1922 Pernod appeared with anise instead of wormwood. Alcohol content is 40 to 43 percent. The normal way to drink pastis is in a tall glass, to which you add ice and water (about five parts water to one part pastis). Various brands of absinthe seem to be making a hit in other pockets of Europe.

Pineau de Charentes (pee-noh duh shah-RAH^NT)

A combination of Cognac and wine, aged two years. A very old process from the Cognac region, whereby the fermentation of wine is stopped by adding Cognac to it. The result is a sweet, fruity flavor. Drink chilled or on the rocks. Lemon is good with it. Only 18 percent alcohol.

Vermouth (vehr-MOOT)

Comes in dry, sweet, and other designations. Very herby. It used to include wormwood, which is "wermut" in German, and evolved to "vermouth" in the Latin countries. The red is sweet and the white is dry. Drink either on the rocks with a lemon twist. Or add a minuscule amount of dry vermouth to gin to get an extra-dry American martini. It's even rumored in the power cocktail set that just thinking about dry vermouth while sipping straight gin makes the perfect extra-dry martini.

Appetizers and Soups

PICTURE YOURSELF in a warm bistro on a cold night, eating a large crock of French onion soup topped with golden, melted *Gruyère* (grew-YEHR). What a sublime experience. Or fresh *foie gras* (fwah GRAH), lightly sautéed, with a glass of *Château d'Yquem* (sha-toh dee-KEHM). That's delicious, too, but very expensive! How about a simple salad of endive and watercress with *Roquefort* (ruck-FOHR)? An onion tart with a glass of white wine?

We hope your palate is piqued. There's something about starters in a French restaurant that gets the appetite up and running, anticipating the wonders yet to come.

Here are some appetizing possibilities.

Do you want to look French? Use your silverware as the French do. No, they're not all left-handed, they just hold their fork in the left hand so they can keep their knife in the right hand. They keep the tines of the fork pointing down, spear the food, and place it in their mouth. The knife is used to cut and also to push food onto the fork. Very important to the French: keep both hands (not elbows) on or above the table at all times. Unlike the American custom of using the right hand for the fork and keeping the left hand on the lap, the French custom accounts for everyone's hands. Those frisky French!

Both *entrée* and *hors d'oeuvres* are used to mean appetizer. In years past, when there were more courses to a meal than there are today, each word had a more specific meaning. Now, individual restaurants determine how to name their courses.

APPETIZERS

Allumettes (ah-lew-MEHT)
Strips of puff pastry baked in the oven with a garnish, such as puréed fish, minced chicken in sauce, or grated cheese. Served as an hors d'oeuvre.

Assiette de Moules Marinières au Muscadet (ah-SYEHT duh MOOL mah-ree-NYEHR oh mew-skah-DEH)
A soup plate of mussels marinières with muscadet wine. *Marinière* is a style that means cooked in white wine, usually with shallots, garlic, and parsley. Used with mussels and sometimes other seafood.

Caviar de Beluga (kah vyahr duh beh-lew-GAH)
You guessed it, Beluga caviar. Those very expensive fish eggs. If you really want it, try some frozen Russian vodka with it.

Délice (day-LEES)
This word is used in old-fashioned French establishments to imply a delectable dish, as in *"délice de Bourgogne"* (day-LEES duh boor-GUH-nyuh), or snails with mushrooms and walnuts. Should you encounter it without any explanation, ask. There is no standard meaning.

Délice de saumon fumé à la mangue (day-LEES duh soh-MOH^N few-MAY ah lah MAH^NG)

Smoked salmon with mango.

Escargots de Bourgogne au Pernod (ehs-kar-GOH duh boor-GUH-nyuh oh pehr-NOH)

Snails in a butter and Pernod sauce with garlic. May be served in the shell or not, depending on the chef. Properly made, the Pernod is subtle, blending very well with the garlic and butter.

Galette (gah-LEHT)

A flat cake made of pastry dough. Much like a tart without sides. Can be anything that a tart can be.

Hors d'oeuvre variés (uhr-DUHV-ruh vah-RYAY)

Assorted appetizers.

Huîtres en coquilles gratinées aux fines herbes (WEE-truh ahⁿ koh-KEE grah-tee-NAY oh feen ZEHRB)

Very likely, this dish is oysters baked with butter, seasoning, and bread crumbs, topped with chopped fresh herbs. Sounds tasty even in English. See *gratin* and *fines herbes* in the glossary. Sometimes you have to ask the waiter exactly how a dish is prepared.

Mesclun (mehs-KLEH^N)

Literally, mixed greens, but in the United States we use it to mean mixed baby greens. Many delicious varieties are used.

Moules marinières (mool mah-ree-NYEHR)

Mussels steamed in herbs and wine.

When eating mussels in France, don't use cutlery to remove the meat from the shell. Instead, use one of the empty shells as a tong to pry the mussel from it. You can also use the shell to scoop up the broth, which is often flavored with wine or a spoonful of fresh cream.

Nage (NAZH)
> A method of preparing shellfish in a broth.

Pan bagnat (pah^n bah-NYAH)
> Canapé with tomatoes, anchovies, and olives.

Pâté (pah-TAY)
> Essentially, a French meatloaf. Various meats are used: pork, veal, duck, goose, venison, and/or rabbit. The meat is ground very fine, seasoned highly, baked, and chilled. *Pâté* is usually served with *cornichons* (kohr-nee-SHOH^N), little sour pickles, and some type of fruit relish, such as lingonberry.

Pâté de campagne (pah-TAY duh kah^m-PAH-nyuh)
> Country-style *pâté*, which usually has meat chunks in it.

Pâté de campagne et confiture d'oignons doux
(pah-TAY duh kah^m-PAH-nyuh eh koh^n-fee-TEWR doh-nyoh^n DOO)
> Country *pâté* served with onion jam (it's not the sort of jam you serve with peanut butter) and condiments (probably *cornichons* and pickled baby onions).

Pâté de foie gras (pah-TAY duh fwah GRAH)
> Pâté made from specially fatted livers of ducks or geese. See *foie gras*.

Pâté en croûte (pah-TAY ah^n KROOT)
> A *pâté* of any type baked in a crust of pie dough.

Pâté maison (pay-TAY meh-ZOH^N)
> House *pâté*.

Saucisson chaud (soh-see-SOH^N SHOH)
> Warm sausage, often a garlic sausage served with mustard and potatoes.

Saumon fumé et sa garniture (soh-MOH^N few-MAY eh sah gahr-nee-TEWR)

Smoked salmon, garnished. Without more information, expect some salad greens and capers, perhaps some horseradish.

Tartare (tahr-TAHR), *à la tartare* (ah lah tahr-TAHR)

Originally used in *steak à la tartare,* or *steak tartare,* which is raw chopped beef with raw eggs and condiments. It's currently a very fashionable term to use with any raw flesh. Thus, *Tartare de Saumon et Vinaigrette de Ciboulette* (tahr-TAHR duh soh-MOH^N eh vee-neh-GREHT duh see-boo-LEHT) is raw salmon chopped up, served with a vinaigrette of chive oil, and garnished (no doubt) with chopped onion, capers, and fresh herbs. A *tartare* is generally eaten with some type of bread.

Tarte à l'oignon (tahrt ah loh-NYOH^N)

An onion tart. Sort of a thin quiche, made with onions and custard. One of André Soltner's traditional specialties, outstanding with a bone-dry white wine.

Tartine (tahr-TEEN)

A slice of bread spread with butter or any other suitable mixture. Actually, an open-faced sandwich. Often served as an appetizer in bistros and cafés.

Terrine de légumes grillés au fromage (teh-REEN duh lay-GEWM gree-YAY oh froh-MAHZH), *Coulis de tomate et gingembre* (koo-LEE duh toh-MAHT eh zheh^n-ZHAH^M-bruh)

A *terrine* (see glossary for discussion of *terrines* and *pâtés*) of grilled vegetables and cheese with a sauce of puréed tomatoes and ginger. Unless there is further information, you'd have to ask what kind of cheese.

SOUPS

Soups can be classified into clear and thickened soups. Clear soups include broths and *consommés.* Thickened soups include *purées,* cream soups, chowders, bisques, and *potages.*

Broths may include garnishes, as in a traditional chicken noodle soup. The most popular French broth-based soup is onion soup. Most clear soups served in restaurants are *consommés*—broths that have been clarified using egg whites and/or ground meat, plus vegetables and herbs. The clarification adds an aesthetic value as well as a more delicate flavor. Many of the names date back to the nineteenth century or earlier. You can memorize them or keep this book with you.

Thickened soups comprise a vast number of styles. Traditional cream soups are puréed, then garnished with the main ingredient. Bisques usually include shellfish, except the famous, old-fashioned tomato bisque. Modern chefs will name almost any creamy, chunky soup "bisque." All sorts of *potages* abound. The term simply means a thick, hearty soup.

Agnès sorel (ah-NYEHS soh-REHL)
 Cream of chicken soup with mushrooms and, often, julienned ox tongue.

Billi Bi (bee-lee BEE)
 Cream of mussel soup.

Bisque de homard (BEESK duh oh-MAHR)
 Lobster bisque.

Consommé (koh^n-soh-MAY)
 Clear soup, usually either chicken or beef, served with various garnishes. The type of *consommé* will be specified. There are many traditional styles, and the name often gives no clue of the garnish.

Consommé à la madrilène (kohⁿ-soh-MAY ah lah mah-dree-LEHN)
> *Consommé* flavored with tomato and served cold.

Consommé à la royale (kohⁿ-soh-MAY ah lah rwah-YAHL)
> Chicken *consommé* garnished with sliced savory custard.

Consommé Brillat-Savarin (kohⁿ-soh-MAY bree-YAH sah-vah-REH^N)
> Chicken *consommé* flavored with celery, with julienned truffles, mushrooms, and carrots.

Consommé brunoise (kohⁿ-soh-MAY brew-NWAHZ)
> *Consommé* garnished with very small diced (*brunoise*) vegetables.

Consommé célestine (kohⁿ-soh-MAY say-lehs-TEEN)
> *Consommé* garnished with strips of *crêpes* mixed with chervil.

Consommé julienne (kohⁿ-soh-MAY zhew-LYEHN)
> *Consommé* garnished with julienned vegetables.

Consommé nesselrode (kohⁿ-soh-MAY neh-sehl-RUHD)
> Game *consommé* with profiteroles filled with chestnut purée and chopped onions and mushrooms.

Consommé printanier (kohⁿ-soh-MAY prehⁿ-tah-NYAY)
> *Consommé* with spring vegetables and chervil.

Petite marmite (puh-TEET mahr-MEET)
> Clear strong broth in a casserole dish.

Potage Crécy (**poh**-TAZH **kray**-SEE)
Purée of carrot soup.

Potage crème de . . . (**poh**-TAZH **krehm duh** . . .)
Cream soup, made with ingredients listed.

Potage crème Dubarry (**poh**-TAZH **krehm dew-bah-**
REE)
Cream of cauliflower soup.

Potage du soir (**poh**-TAZH **dew** SWAHR)
Same idea as *soupe du jour,* but this one means
"*potage* (thick, hearty soup) of the evening."

Potage Parmentier (**poh**-TAZH **pahr-mah^n-**TYAY)
Purée of potato and leek soup.

Potage Saint-Germain (**poh**-TAZH **se^n zhehr-**MEH^N)
Purée of fresh pea soup.

Soupe à l'oignon (**soop ah loh-**NYOH^N)
Onion soup, usually baked with croutons and
grated Gruyère.

Soupe au chou (**soop oh** SHOO)
Cabbage soup.

Soupe du jour (**soop dew** ZHOOR)
This means "soup of the day."

Vichyssoise (**vee-shee-**SWAHZ)
Chilled cream of potato and leek soup.

? DID YOU KNOW?
Despite its French appellation, *vichyssoise* is a dis-
tinctly American soup invented at the Ritz Carlton in
Boston by French chef Louis Diat in the early part of the
century (the exact date is not known).

Breads

TO BREAK BREAD IN FRANCE carries almost religious implications. As in the rest of Europe and most of the world, wheat bread is truly the staff of life. Expect excellent bread in a French restaurant, and don't hesitate to question mediocre offerings.

If you get a long piece of uncut bread, simply break off pieces as you desire; that's the French way.

Baguette (bah-GEHT)
Long, thin loaf of French bread. Literally, "stick." Also used to mean "chopstick."

Bâtard (bah-TAHR)
A large loaf of French bread, bigger around than a *baguette*.

Brioche (bree-YUSH)
Rich bread made with plenty of butter and eggs. This is the word that Marie Antoinette used in her famous saying: "Let them eat brioche." (No kidding.)

Pain (PEH^N)
Bread.

Pain de mie (PEH^N duh MEE)
Sandwich bread.

Salads

IN TRADITIONAL FRENCH DINING, where a salad is one course among many, the salad is generally mixed greens with a vinaigrette. It may be garnished with a tomato or some other raw vegetable, but it is mostly greens. In less formal situations, however, the salad is a much more involved course, sometimes the main course of a light supper or lunch. There are many delicious standards, as well as new inventions every day. Some of these salads are wonderful with wine, others seem better suited to beer or mineral water, if you prefer. All are good with a hearty, crusty bread. Don't assume the salad will be a low-fat alternative, as some of these include high-fat ingredients. They're scrumptious, though.

In France the salad is served after the main course as a means to settle the stomach and cleanse the palate. Both a fork and knife are used to eat the salad.

Grosses asperges en saison à l'huile de truffe et parmesan (GRUHS ah-SPEHRZH ahⁿ seh-ZOH^N ah lweel duh TREWF eh pahr-mah-SAH^N)
Salad of large asparagus with truffle oil and parmesan cheese.

Jeune salade du jardin (zhuhn sah-lahd dew zhahr-DEH^N)

Mixed baby greens.

Salade niçoise (sah-lahd nee-SWAHZ)

An arrangement of tomatoes, cucumbers, peppers, onions, hard-boiled eggs, black (niçoise) olives, tuna, anchovies, and vinaigrette.

Salade d'épinards aux foies de volailles (sah-lahd day-pee-NAHR oh fwah duh voh-LIE)

Salad of spinach and chicken livers (with a vinaigrette, if not otherwise stated).

Médaillon de chèvre chaud aux graines de sésame et tomates rôties (may-die-YOH^N duh SHEH-vruh shoh oh grehn duh say-ZAHM eh toh-MAHT roh-TEE)

Medallions of goat cheese with sesame seeds and roasted tomatoes.

Salade d'endive et de cresson au roquefort (sah-lahd dahⁿ-DEEV eh duh kruh-SOH^N oh ruck-FOHR)

Belgian endive (the white little bunches) and watercress salad with Roquefort cheese. This is typically French: a rich cheese on a salad of two very bitter greens. It creates a wonderful dynamic interplay of sensations on the taste buds.

Traditional French restaurants haven't been too good for vegetarians, but more and more are offering special vegetarian sections on the menu. If the restaurant doesn't list any vegetarian items, phone ahead and request that the chef prepare one for you. As long as you give enough lead time, there should be no problem.

Salade de caille au foie gras (sah-lahd duh KIE oh fwah GRAH)

> Salad of quail and *foie gras*. A very typical bistro dish.

Salade frisée aux lardons (sah-lahd free-ZAY oh lar-DOH^N)

> Curly endive salad with small strips of crisp bacon and a vinaigrette dressing. Often served with a poached egg on top. A real traditional dish.

Salade mesclun (sah-lahd mehs-KLEH^N)

> Mixed greens with vinaigrette.

I NEED . . .

Puis-j'avoir . . . PWEEZH ah-VWAHR . . .	*Can I have* . . .
une serviette? ewn sehrv-YEHT?	*a napkin?*
une fourchette? ewn foor-SHEHT?	*a fork?*
une cuillère? ewn kwee-YEHR?	*a spoon?*
un couteau? eh^n koo-TOH?	*a knife?*

Entrées

AT ONE TIME, the entrée was one among several courses, but its meaning has changed over time, and today it generally refers to the appetizer in France and the main course in the United States. Sometimes on French menus appetizers will be listed as *"Hors d'oeuvre."* Even as we begin our discussion of entrées, there is a significant movement in the restaurant industry to downplay the idea of a main course and instead offer plates of various sizes from which the customers can pick and choose. The idea comes from the Spanish *tapas* but has spread into many styles of restaurants. Most French restaurants still offer distinct courses, particularly at dinner, but don't be surprised to find some that simply list "small plates," "medium plates," and "large plates." Often, a diner is expected to have more than one plate, and just as often it is expected that people will share the plates. The trend is just beginning, and it will be interesting to see how it develops. Will the French menu evolve once again?

MEAT AND POULTRY ENTRÉES

Alouette à la paysanne (ah-LWEHT ah lah peh-ee-ZAHN)
Lark with bacon, onions, and potatoes.

Boeuf à la mode (BUHF ah lah MUHD)
Rump of beef braised with vegetables in red wine.

Canard rôti à l'orange (kah-NAR roh-TEE ah loh-RAH^{N}ZH)
Roast duck with an orange sauce. A rather old-fashioned dish.

Canard montmorency (moh^n-mohr-ah^n-SEE)
Duck with cherry sauce, named after a type of cherry grown near Paris. Not much newer-fashioned than duck with orange sauce, although both are quite tasty.

Caneton aux navets et petits oignons (kahn-TOH^N oh nah-VEH eh puh-TEE zoh-NYOH^N)
Duckling with turnips and little onions.

Carré d'agneau grillé (kah-RAY dah-NOYH gree-YAY)
Grilled lamb chops.

HOW DO YOU LIKE YOUR MEAT COOKED?

bleu	BLUH	*very rare*
saignant	seh-NYAH^N	*rare*
à point	ah PWAH^N	*medium*
bien cuit	byeh^n kwee	*well done*

Carré d'agneau persillé (pehr-zee-YAY)
Rack of lamb, roasted and coated with a bit of mustard and a mixture of chopped parsley and garlic, served with the natural juices or a wine sauce.

Cassoulet (kah-soo-LEH)
A white bean casserole made with a combination of several meats: goose, duck, pork, sausages, lamb, and/or mutton. Hearty and filling.

Chevreuil en croûte de fenouil et pistaches (sheh-VRUHY ah^n KROOT duh fuh-NOOY eh pee-STAHSH)
Venison in a crust of fennel seed and pistachios.

Choucroute alsacienne (shoo-KROOT ahl-sah-SYEHN)
Sauerkraut with salt pork, ham, and sausages. Typical dish for the Alsace region.

Coq au vin (kuck oh VEH^N)
Rooster (or just chicken) in red wine.

Côte de veau grillée et purée de pomme de terre à l'ail (kuht duh VOH gree-YAY eh pew-RAY duh puhm duh TEHR ah LIE)
Grilled veal chop with garlic mashed potatoes.

Foie de veau poêlé (fwah duh voh pwah-LAY)
Calf's liver, pan-fried.

Rognon de veau moutardier flambé grande fine (roh-NYOH^N duh voh moo-tahr-DYAY flah^m-BAY grah^{n}d FEEN)
Veal kidneys with mustard, flamed with Cognac.

Langue de boeuf à la bourgeoise (lah^{n}g duh BUHF ah lah boor-ZHWAHZ)
Beef tongue in red wine with bacon and carrots.

Gratin de ris de veau (grah-TEH^N duh ree duh VOH)
A casserole of sweetbreads (the thymus gland of the veal). Sweetbreads are like extra-rich sea scallops, delicious but very high in cholesterol.

Magret de canard (mah-GREH duh kah-NAHR)
  Duck breast, grilled only until it's still rare, sliced very thin. Often served with peppery and/or fruity sauces.

Magret de canard et macedoine de riz et légume et sauce shiitake (eh mahs-DWAHN duh ree eh lay-GEWM eh sohs shee-tah-KEH)
  Breast of duck with shiitake mushroom sauce and mixed vegetables and rice.

Navarin (nah-vah-REH^N)
  Lamb stew.

Oie en daube normande (wah ah^n dohb nohr-MAH^{N}D)
  Goose stuffed with pork, bacon, apples, braised vegetables, and cider.

Poularde rôtie au jus (poo-LAHRD roh-tee oh ZHEW)
  Roast chicken with natural juices.

Poulet à la provençale (poo-LEH ah lah proh-veh^u-SAHL)
  Chicken cooked with
  olive oil, garlic, and
  tomatoes, perhaps basil.
  These are the traditional
  ingredients from Provence.

Rôti de boeuf au jus (roo-TEE duh BUHF oh ZHEW)
  Roast beef served with its natural juices.

Steak au poivre (stehk oh PWAH vruh)
  Black pepper–coated steak, served with a Cognac and démi-glace sauce.

Steak-frites (stehk FREET)
  A strip steak with shoestring French fries.

> " *A certain nervousness is always associated with the wine-tasting part of the evening. Once in a while, a man who is trying to impress his date will turn up his nose at perfectly fine wine, with a comment like: 'Ce ne'st pas belle de coeur.' (It has no heart.) We really don't mind, as it's all part of the job. All it means is that the waiters will be enjoying some really good wine after the customers are gone!*
>
> JOHN PAUL PICOT, OWNER,
> LA BONNE SOUPE, NEW YORK "

Suprème de volaille aux petits légumes, beurre de ciboulette (sew-PREHM duh voh-LIE oh puh-TEE lay-GEWM buhr duh see-boo-LEHT)

Sautéed breast of chicken (or hen or capon), baby vegetables, chive butter.

Tournedos de boeuf aux cinq poivres (toor-nuh-DOH duh BUHF oh sehⁿk PWAH-vruh)

Thin slices of beef tenderloin with a five-pepper sauce (white, black, pink, green, red).

SEAFOOD ENTRÉES

Bouillabaisse (bwee-yah-BEHZ)

Seafood and fish soup. Often served with a dab of *rouille*, a garlicky mayonnaise-type sauce, and garlic croutons.

Coquilles Saint-Jacques Mornay (koh-KEE seⁿ ZHAHK mohr-NAY)

Scallops baked in a white wine and cream sauce, with some grated cheese, gratinéed. Often served in scallop shells with a border of duchesse potatoes.

Crevettes grillées au beurre blanc de cerfeuil et cous-cous (kruh-VEHT gree-YAY oh buhr blah^n duh sehr-FOY eh koos-KOOS)

 Grilled shrimp (or prawns) with chervil *beurre blanc* and couscous.

Filet de sole meunière (fee-LAY duh SUHL muh-NYEHR)

 Sautéed fillet of sole or flounder, with a brown butter and lemon sauce. A very simple and tradi-tional French method of preparing sole. Dover sole would be the best choice.

Homard sauté à la julienne d'artichauts et truffes (oh-MAHR soh-TAY ah lah zhew-LYEHN dahr-tee-SHOH eh TREWF)

 Lobster sautéed with julienne artichokes and truffles.

Lotte poêlée au verjus et fenouil confit (luht pwah-LAY oh vehr-ZHEW ch fuh-NOOY koh^n-FEE)

 Monkfish, pan-fried, with verjus and fennel confit.

Saumon en croûte de graine de sésame et sauce d'épinard (soh-MOH^N ah^n KROOT duh grehn duh say-ZAHM eh sohs day-pee-NAR)

 Salmon with a sesame-seed crust and a spinach sauce.

Saumon en papillote (soh-MOH^N ah^n pah-pee-YEHT)

 Salmon baked in parchment paper with season-ings and garnishes. When the pouch comes to the table, it should be puffed up, and when it's cut open the aromas should escape to your nostrils.

Luncheon and Lighter Items, Sides, Bistro and Café Fare

Asperges villeroi (ahs-PEHRZH veel-RWAH)
  White asparagus tips with truffle and ham sauce.

Assiette de crudités (ah-SYEHT de krew-dee-TAY)
  A plate of raw vegetables.

Croque monsieur (kruhk muh-SYUH)
  Grilled or baked ham and cheese sandwich, usually open-faced.

Frites (FREET)
  French fries.

Oeufs cocotte à la crème (UH koh-KUHT ah lah KREHM)
  Eggs baked in their own dish with cream.

Omelette aux champignons (ohm-LEHT oh shah^m-pee-NYOH^N)
  Mushroom omelette.

Omelette fines herbes (ohm-LEHT feen ZEHRB)
  Omelette with chopped parsley.

Pain grillé (peh^n gree-YAY)
  Toast.

Pommes duchesse (puhm dew-SHEHS)
  Puréed potatoes mixed with eggs, baked. Often piped through a pastry bag in a decorative border.

Pommes frites (puhm FREET)
  French fries.

Pommes gaufrettes (**puhm goh-**FREHT)

Waffle potatoes, fried. They're very thin like potato chips, not like the frozen seasoned things found in so many places today.

Pommes dauphinoise (**puhm doh-fee-**NWAHZ)

Potato slices baked with a custard and grated Gruyère cheese.

Pot-au-feu (**poh-toh-**FUH)

Boiled beef and vegetables. Much tastier than it sounds. First you eat the broth, then savor the meat and vegetables. An old French tradition.

Ratatouille (**rah-tah-**TOO-ee)

Stew of eggplant, squashes, bell peppers, tomatoes, garlic, and olive oil.

When a French diner has finished the meal, he or she puts the fork and knife on the plate at an angle, stretching from ten o'clock to four o'clock, with the fork tines pointing down. In fact, a French waiter (in France) may not clear your plate if you don't follow this convention. It's a nice thing to know.

Desserts and Sweets

DESSERTS (deh-SEHR) or *entremets* (ahⁿ-truh-MEH) can make or break the entire dining experience. Like most cultures, the French adore sweets, and they create some wonderful desserts. If you dine in France, you'll notice that having two desserts is not unusual, the second most likely involving chocolate. One second dessert you may be served is called *mignardises* (mee-nyahr-DEEZ). These are small, sweet delicacies, often made with chocolate.

Currently, new desserts are popping up all over the place. It seems that desserts are being created faster than any other menu item. Listed below are some of the standards, but you can expect all sorts of innovative ideas. The more daring you are, the bigger chance of an unforgettable experience. At any rate, save room for dessert. You'll be glad you did.

 Remember, if you like dessert wines, that chocolate overpowers and neutralizes them. With chocolate, drink coffee and/or Cognac or a liqueur.

Baies fraîches de saison (beh frehsh duh seh-ZOHⁿ)
Seasonal fresh berries.

Bavarois (bah-vah-RWAH)
Bavarian cream, which is made from custard, gelatin, and whipped cream.

Beignet (beh-NYEH)
> Fritter or doughnut.

Blancmange (blah^n-MAH^{N}ZH)
> An almond-flavored sweet gelatin dessert.

Compote (koh^m-POHT)
> Stewed fruit.

Coupe (KOOP)
> Sundae.

Crème anglaise (krehm ah^n-GLEHZ)
> Custard sauce. This is the most common dessert sauce in the French repertoire. It's made from milk, vanilla, sugar, and egg yolks, cooked over a double boiler until it coats the back of a spoon. It can be flavored with any number of choices, but vanilla is always there. It is safe to say that without *crème anglaise* there would be no French dessert making.

Crème brûlée (krehm brew-LAY)
> A very rich custard that is coated with sugar and caramelized.

Crème brûlée aux fruits rouges (krehm brew-LAY oh FRWEE ROOZH)
> *Crème brûlée* with red berries.

Crème caramel (krehm kah-rah-MEHL) or *Flan* (FLAH^N)
> A custard that is baked on top of caramelized sugar. When served, it is inverted so the caramel is on top. Similar to *crème brûlée*, but the custard is less rich, and the caramel is more extensive, actually saucy, and darker than in the *brûlée*.

Dacquoise (dah-KWAHZ)
> A layered cake made from hazelnut meringues filled with French buttercream. Although very rich, it feels extremely light on the palate.

Gâteau (gah-TOH)
   Cake.

Gâteau quatre quarts (gah-TOH kah-truh KAHR)
   Pound cake.

Gâteau Saint-Honoré (gah-TOH seh^n-toh-noh-RAY)
   A showy cake with a pastry base topped with cream puffs filled with pastry cream, whipped cream, and drizzled caramel.

Gaufre au chocolat et noisettes, glace à la vanille
(GOH-fruh oh shoh-koh-LAH eh nwah-ZET, glas ah lah vah-NEE)
   Waffle with chocolate and hazelnuts, topped with vanilla ice cream.

Genoise (zhuh-NWAHZ)
   Sponge cake.

Glace (GLAS)
   Ice cream.

Langue de chat (lah^{n}g duh SHAH)
   Don't get upset, it's not *really* a cat's tongue—it's actually a long, thin biscuit that might *resemble* a cat's tongue. Generally served with liqueurs or ice cream. The batter can also be used to make those cute little dessert cups for holding mousses, puddings, and ices.

Melba (mehl-BAH)
   Raspberry sauce.

Mont blanc (moh^n BLAH^N)
   Puréed chestnut and whipped cream dessert.

Mousse au chocolat (moos oh shoh-koh-LAH)
   Chocolate mousse. A dessert of chocolate, cream, eggs, and often whipped egg whites. Although the word means foam, the dessert is seldom light and airy. It's usually dense and chocolaty. Yum. An old standard that holds its own.

Nantais (nahⁿ-TEH)
Small almond biscuits.

Napoléon (nah-poh-lay-OH^N)
Puff pastry layers filled with pastry cream.

Napoléon de fruits sur pâte feuilletée croustillante, coulis de mangues et framboises (nah-poh-lay-ohⁿ duh FRWEE sewr paht foy-yeh-TAY croo-STEE-yant, koo-LEE duh mahⁿg eh frah^m-BWAHZ)
Napoleon of fruit made with crispy puff pastry, served with a *coulis* (purée) of mangos and raspberries.

Notre sélection de glaces et sorbets (NUH-truh say-leh-KSYOH^N duh glas eh sohr-BEH)
Our selection of ice cream and sorbet (water-based sherbet).

Oeufs à la neige (uh ah lah NEHZH)
Meringue "eggs" on crème anglaise.

Omelette norvégienne (ohm-LEHT nohr-vay-ZHYEHN)
Baked Alaska: A mound of ice cream sandwiched between sponge cake and covered with meringue. It's baked in a very hot oven until browned. The baking time is short enough that the ice cream doesn't melt. Then it is sprinkled with a liquor of choice and flambéed.

Oreilles de cochon (oh-RAY duh koh-SHOH^N)
Pig's Ears (sugared puff pastry in the shape of a pig's ear).

Paris–brest (pah-ree BREHST)
Ring of *pâte à choux* filled with cream, almonds, and almond paste. Named after the bicycle race, the ring representing a wheel.

Pêche melba (pesh mehl-BAH)
Vanilla ice cream with peaches and raspberry sauce.

Petites bananes rôties au four à la vanille et rhum, glace à la cacahuètes (put-TEET bah-NAHN roh-TEE oh foor ah lah vah-NEE eh RUHM, glahs ah lah kah-kah-WET)

Oven-roasted baby bananas with vanilla and rum, with peanut ice cream.

Petits fours (puh-tee FOOR)

Small cakes, pastries, and tarts.

Pomme au four aux épices (puhm oh FOOR oh zay-PEES)

Spice baked apple.

Profiteroles au chocolat (proh-fee-tuh-ROHL oh shoh-koh-LAH)

Profiteroles (small cream-puff shells) filled with ice cream and/or whipped cream, drizzled with chocolate.

Sabayon (sah-bah-YOH^N)

Custard of egg yolk and wine. From the Italian *zabaglione.*

Sorbet (sohr-BEH)

Frozen confection based on fruit juice and/or purée. A water ice, or water-based sherbet.

Tarte au chocolat mi-amère, biscuit au chocolat et à la pistache, glace au chocolat (tahrt oh sho-koh-LAH mee ah-MEHR, bees-kwee oh shoh-koh-LAH eh ah lah pee-STASH, glas oh shoh-koh-LAH)

Bittersweet Chocolate Torte, Chocolate and Pistachio Biscuit, Chocolate Ice Cream.

Tarte aux fruits
(tart oh FRWEE)
Fruit tart.

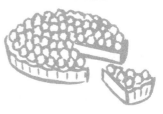

Tarte à l'orange caramelisée, glace à la vanille,
sauce au chocolat (**tahrt ah loh-RAH^NZH kar-ah-meh-**
lee-ZAY, glas ah lah vah-NEE, sohs oh shoh-koh-LAH)
Caramelized Orange Tart, Vanilla Ice Cream,
Chocolate Sauce.

Tarte aux pommes (**tahrt oh PUHM**)
Apple tart.

Tarte tatin (**tahrt tah-TEH^N**)
Caramelized apple tart.

CHECK, PLEASE!

L'addition, s'il vous plaît.	*The check, please.*
l'ah-dee-SYOH^N, see voo PLEH.	
Est-ce que le service est compris?	*Is service included?*
ehs kuh luh sehr-VEES eh koh^m-PREE?	
Il y a une erreur.	*There's a mistake.*
eel YAH ewn eh-RUHR	
C'est pour vous.	*This is for you.*
seh poor VOO.	

Wines and After-Dinner Drinks

WINES

A MEAL WITHOUT WINE is somehow just not complete. To the French, it's blasphemy. If you're uncomfortable with a wine list, ask the server for a recommendation. This usually works fine. If the price is too high, ask for a less expensive recommendation. If the server asks whether you're considering white or red, ask him or her for a recommendation. That is how you can make sure that you get a reasonably good wine without knowing much except the price.

SELECTING A WINE

Pourriez vous me recommandez un bon vin . . .		Could you recommend a good . . . wine?
Poo-ree-yeh VOO muh ruh-koh-mahⁿ-DEH uhⁿ bohⁿ vehⁿ . . .		
rouge	ROOZH	*red*
blanc	BLAHᴺ	*white*
doux	DOO	*sweet*
sec	SEHK	*dry*
léger	leh-ZHEH	*light*

But you want more control than that. So here's a primer on how to order wine, and just a bit about French wine. Please investigate wines at every opportunity. There's an unlimited amount to learn, but the pursuit is so pleasurable.

Drink white wine with seafoods, white meats, and vegetarian dishes with light sauces. There's a reason for this: white wines tend not to overpower these light-bodied and delicately flavored foods. Red wines go well with red meats and heavier foods, such as tomato sauces and fattier items like dark fish.

To match the style of wine with the type of food is another consideration. Acidic foods, such as tomato-based sauces, go well with fairly acidic and fairly dry wines (such as a no-oak chardonnay or a pinot grigio with a *sole meunière*), and sweet foods call for sweet wines (such as a semi-dry riesling with bread pudding). Sweeter wines also do well with smoked or salty foods.

Red meats call not just for red wine, but for full-bodied, complex, tannic red wine. The simple but rich aspect of red meat calls for a complex red wine to enhance it. Foods that call for complex white wines, such as full-bodied, oaky chardonnay, include rich white and cheesy sauces and roasted white meats.

Remember that French wines don't list the grape variety. Rather, they rely on regions and estates to identify the type of wine. As a short reminder, here are the major wine regions of France with the grape varieties they use.

Alsace (ahl-ZAHS)

Here we see only white wines. The most popular grapes used are riesling, gewürztraminer, and sylvaner.

Bordeaux (bohr-DOH)

Red wines are a blend of cabernet sauvignon, cabernet franc, and merlot; whites are a blend of sauvignon blanc and semillon.

Burgundy (Bourgogne, boor-GUH-nyuh)

Red wines are from the pinot noir, and whites are chardonnays. Beaujolais (boh-zhoh-LEH), a subregion in southern Burgundy, uses the gamay grape to produce a light, fruity wine. Chablis (shah-BLEE) is another subregion, producing white wines from chardonnay. They are dry, flinty, fruity wines.

Loire (LWAHR)

The region is known primarily for its whites using the sauvignon blanc grape and for a hearty red from the cabernet franc, Chinon.

Rhône (ROHN)

The primary grape for reds is syrah, and whites are uncommon here. The most famous Rhône wine is Châteauneuf-du-Pape, a blend of some thirteen grape varieties.

" *The general principles for choosing wines are whites with seafood and poultry, reds with meat. However, there are always exceptions to these rules. You should always enjoy your favorite wine with your favorite meal and not worry so much about making the conventional choice.*

MICHAEL SMITH, WAITER,
OCEAN AVENUE SEAFOOD, LOS ANGELES "

AFTER-DINNER DRINKS

There are basically three types of after-dinner drinks: *brandies, eaux de vie,* and *liqueurs.* The great brandies include Cognacs and Armagnacs. These are distilled from wine and aged. *Eaux de vie* are distilled from fruits other than grapes. And *liqueurs* are sweetened drinks made from distilled spirits.

Cognac

Cognacs range in price from a few dollars to more than a hundred dollars a glass. Armagnacs are similarly priced. Both names refer to regions, and only specified brandy from that region can be called by the regional appellation. The best way to tell the quality in the restaurant is by the price.

Eaux de Vie

Eaux de Vie (oh-duh-VEE) include *poire* (pwahr) *William,* from pears; *calvados* (kahl-vah-DOHS), from apples; *framboise* (frah^m-BWAHZ), from raspberries; and *Mirabelle* (mee-rah-BEHL), from plums. There are many others. Unless the bottle says "liqueur," these are high-proof spirits with only a touch of aroma from the original fruit. Many are drunk chilled.

Liqueurs

Liqueurs include *Grand Marnier* (grah^n mahr-NYAY), orange flavored, made with Cognac; *Bénédictine* (bay-nay-deek-TEEN), made with herbs; *Chambord* (chah^m-BOHR), flavored with raspberry, *Cointreau* (kwah^n-TROH) flavored with orange; *Mandarine Napoléon* (mah^ndah-REEN nah-poh-lay-OH^N), with tangerine; and *Crème de menthe* (krehm duh MAH^NT), with mint. Again, liqueurs number in the hundreds, and only your sense of adventure dictates how many you wish to try.

Coffee

THE FRENCH DRINK a great deal of coffee. After dinner, after all the desserts are eaten, coffee is commonly served with an after-dinner drink and a cigar. In French restaurants in the United States, you won't have to wait until dessert is cleared to get your coffee; you can have it alongside your dessert. If you expect coffee with your dessert in France, go ahead and ask for it, but expect some sort of disapproval from the server, even to the point of ignoring your request. They like to stick to their customs.

The coffee drunk at night is often espresso, but with a lighter roast—dubbed "French" roast—than the very dark roast used in Italy. Espresso is a method of making coffee—fast—as its name suggests. Hot water under pressure is forced through coffee to produce a strong cup of coffee. Just as likely as coffee made by the espresso method is filtered coffee, again using a "French" roast. In some places, you may be served a plunger-type coffee maker, known as a French press, at the table.

Café au lait, cappuccino, and *café crème* are breakfast beverages in France and not generally offered at night. But French restaurants in the United States commonly offer such coffees, just as they offer regular "American" coffee.

Café au lait

Café au lait is French coffee with lots of hot milk. The milk and coffee are poured into the cup simultaneously to mix them. At home, the coffee will probably be filtered or brewed in a plunger-type coffee maker. In cafés and most restaurants, an espresso machine will be used.

Café crème

Café crème is technically with cream rather than milk, and the cream is added in smaller quantities to the cup of coffee, not put into the cup simultaneously with the coffee. But the terms are often used interchangeably, and there are many slight variations on how milk and/or cream are combined with the coffee.

Cappuccino

Cappuccino is an Italian beverage made by floating steamed milk foam on top of espresso.

Most French restaurants in the United States will have a standard espresso machine and will make espresso and cappuccino, as well as standard "American" coffee. Some use the French press, which makes a nice tableside presentation. Whatever type of coffee you choose, try an after-dinner drink, just to end the dinner on a special note.

TIPPING

Most French restaurants include a 10 to 15 percent service charge on the bill. It's not uncommon to add on a little something—ranging from 2 to 3 dollars—if the patron is satisfied with the quality of the food and the service.

GLOSSARY OF INGREDIENTS AND TECHNIQUES

Cooking Terms and Techniques and Miscellaneous Culinary Lingo

À point (ah pWAH^N)
Rare, as in steak.

Assiette (ah-SYEHT)
Plate.

Bon appétit. (boh nah-pay-TEE.)
Enjoy your meal. It means literally "good appetite." The appropriate response is "merci."

Charcuterie (chahr-kew-TREE)
The production of pâtés, terrines, galantines, sausages, and similar foods.

Clamart, à la (klah-MAHR)
Served with green peas.

Flambé (flah^m-BAY)
Flamed, usually tableside.

Gratin (grah-TEH^N)
Means the thin crust that forms on food when heated under a broiler. Often it implies cheese and/or bread crumbs as part of that crust. "Au gratin" means food prepared in this way.

Julienne (zhew-LYEHN)
Very thin strips of vegetables or meat.

Menu table d'hôte (muh-new tah-bluh DOHT)

A menu in which the price of the entrée includes a complete meal. Only the entrée selections will have a price. Very rare these days.

> **DID YOU KNOW?**
> Auguste Escoffier (1846–1935) is often called "the king of chefs and the chef of kings." He established the modern menu sequence and standardized many traditional recipes. His *Guide Culinaire*, first published in 1903 and revised many times before his death, is still a dominant authority for the professional kitchen. It demonstrates that the modern mentality of simplicity in cooking has roots at least a hundred years old. It's still the rule in Western kitchens to refer to *Le Guide Culinaire* to see what Escoffier has to say on a particular issue.

Normande, à la (nohr-MAH^{N}D)

Fish sauce with cream and eggs.

Petit déjeuner (puh-tee day-zhuh-NAY)

Breakfast.

Poêlé (pwah-LAY)

Modern menus frequently use this term to mean either "pan-seared "or "pan-fried." Escoffier has the more narrow definition of cooking with a small amount of fat in the oven, in a covered pan.

Prix Fixe (pree-FEEX)

Fixed-price menu for complete meals.

Sauté (soh-TAY)

Cooked in a small amount of fat, usually clarified butter or good oil, at a relatively high heat.

Meats and Poultry

Agneau (ah-NYOH)

Lamb.

Aiguillette (eh-gee-YEHT)

Thin slices of breast of poultry.

Aiguillette de Boeuf (eh-gee-YEHT duh BUHF)
Rump roast of beef.

Alouette (ah-LWEHT)
Lark.

Andouille (ah^n-DOO-ee)
Smoked sausage from pork.

Boudin (boo-DEH^N)
Blood sausage.

Caille (KIE)
Quail.

Canard (kah-NAHR)
Duck.

Caneton (kahn-TOH^N)
Duckling.

Carré d'Agneau (kah-ray dah-NYOH)
Rack of lamb.

Carré de Porc (kah-ray duh POHR)
Pork loin.

Cervelles (sehr-VEHL)
Brains.

Chateaubriand (shah-toh-bree-AH^N)
The center cut of the tenderloin (filet) of beef. Often broiled for two, served with a *béarnaise* sauce and a *bouquetière* (assortment) of vegetables.

Cochon (koh-SHOH^N)
Pig.

Coeur de Boeuf (kuhr duh BUHF)
Beef heart.

Contre Filet (koh^n-truh fee-LAY)
Sirloin steak.

Coq (KUHK)
Rooster.

Côte (KUHT)
Rib (see *côtelette*).

Côtelette (kuht-LET)
Chop (as in pork chop, lamb chop). The terms *côte* and *côtelette* are sometimes used interchangeably, although the cut is always from the rib or loin.

Cuisses de Grenouilles (kwees duh gruh-NOO-yuh)
Frog legs.

Dinde (DEH^ND)
Turkey.

Entrecôte (ah^n-truh-KUHT)
Sirloin or rib steak.

Escalope (ays-kah-LUHP)
Cutlet.

Escargot (ays-kahr-GOH)
Snails.

Faisan (fuh-ZAH^N)
Pheasant.

Filet de Boeuf (fee-leh duh BUHF)
Tenderloin (or filet) of beef.

Foie (FWAH)
Liver.

Foie Gras (fwah-GRAH)
Fatted liver (duck or goose). Made fat by feeding the animal excessive quantities of grains.

Gigot (d'Agneau) (zhee-goh dah-NYOH)
Leg of lamb.

Jambon (zhah^m-BOH^N)
Ham.

Langue (LAH^NG)
Tongue.

Lapin (lah-PEH^N)
Rabbit.

Moelle (MWAHL)
Bone marrow.

Mou de Veau (moo duh VOH)
Calf's lungs.

Oie (WAH)
Goose.

Ours (OORS)
Bear.

Palombe (pah-LOH^{M}B)
Wild dove.

Pieds de Porc (pyeh duh POHR)
Pig's feet.

Poitrine (pwah-TREEN)
Breast.

Poularde (poo-LAHRD)
Hen (roasting chicken).

Queue de Boeuf (kuh duh BUHF)
Oxtail.

Ris de Veau (ree duh VOH)
Sweetbreads (thymus gland of the calf).

Rognon (roh-NYOH^N)
Kidneys.

Rognon de Veau (roh-nyoh^n duh VOH)
Veal kidneys.

Saucisse (soh-SEES)
Sausage.

Saucisson (soh-see-SOH^N)
Large sausage.

Seafood

Anchois (ah^n-SHWAH)
Anchovy.

Bar (BAHR)
Sea bass.

Brochet (broh-SHEH)
Pike (fish).

Coquilles Saint-Jacques (koh-kee seⁿ ZHAHK)
  Scallops.

Crevettes (kruh-VEHT)
  Shrimp.

Écrevisse (ay-kruh-VEES)
  Crayfish.

Églefin (ay-gluh-FEH^N)
  Haddock.

Fruits de mer (frwee duh-MEHR)
  Seafood.

Hareng (ah-RAH^N)
  Herring.

Homard (oh-MAHR)
  Lobster.

Huîtres (WEE-truh)
  Oysters.

Lotte (LUHT)
  Monkfish.

Loup (LOO)
  Sea bass.

Moules (MOOL)
  Mussels.

Oursins (oor-SEH^N)
  Sea urchins.

Palourdes (pah-LOOR)
  Clams.

Poisson (pwah-SOH^N)
  Fish.

Saumon (soh-MOH^N)
  Salmon.

Saumon Fumé (soh-MOH^N few-MAY)
  Smoked salmon.

Thon (TOH^N)
  Tuna.

Truite (TRWEET)
Trout.

Vegetables and Fruits

Ail (EYE)
Garlic.

Ananas (ah-nah-NAH)
Pineapple.

Artichaut (ahr-tee-SHOH)
Artichoke.

Asperges (ah-SPEHRZH)
Asparagus.

Aubergines (oh-behr-ZHEEN)
Eggplant. Aubergine to the English.

Betteraves (beh-TRAHV)
Beets.

Carottes (kah-RUHT)
Carrots.

Céleri (sayl-REE)
Celery.

Céleri-rave (sayl-ree RAHV)
Celery root (celeriac)

Cèpes (SEHP)
Wild mushrooms, same as Porcini.

Cerises (suh-REES)
Cherries.

Champignons (shah^m-pee-NYOH^N)
Mushrooms.

Chanterelle (shah^n-TREHL)
Wild mushroom, yellow.

Choucroute (shoo-KROOT)
Sauerkraut.

Chou-fleur (shoo-FLUHR)
Cauliflower.

Citron *(see-TROH^N)*
Lemon.

Citron vert *(see-TROH^N VEHR)*
Lime.

Coeur d'artichaut *(kuhr dahr-tee-SHOH)*
Artichoke heart.

Concombre *(koh^n-KOH^M-bruh)*
Cucumber.

Échalote *(ay-shah-LUHT)*
Shallot.

Épinards *(ay-pee-NAHR)*
Spinach

Figue *(FEEG)*
Fig.

Flageolets *(fluh-zhoh-LEH)*
Dried beans.

Fonds d'artichauts *(foh^n dahr-tee-SHOH)*
Artichoke bottoms.

Fraises *(FREHZ)*
Strawberries.

Framboises *(frah^m-BWAHZ)*
Raspberries.

Haricots *(ah-ree-KOH)*
Beans.

Haricots verts *(ah-ree-koh VEHR)*
Green beans.

Laitue *(leh-TEW)*
Lettuce.

Marrons *(mah-ROH^N)*
Chestnuts.

Morels *(moh-REHL)*
Very woody wild mushrooms. They look like little human brains.

Navets *(nah-VEH)*
Turnips.

Pamplemousse *(pah^m-pluh-MOOS)*
Grapefruit.

Pêche *(PESH)*
Peach.

Persil *(pehr-SEE)*
Parsley.

Poireaux *(pwah-ROH)*
Leeks.

Pois *(PWAH)*
Peas.

Pommes *(PUHM)*
Apples.

Pommes de terre *(puhm duh TEHR)*
Potatoes.

Radis *(rah-DEE)*
Radish.

Raifort *(reh-FOHR)*
Horseradish.

Raisins *(reh-ZEH^N)*
Grapes.

Riz *(REE)*
Rice.

Tomates *(toh-MAHT)*
Tomatoes.

Truffe *(TREWF)*
Truffles. An underground fungus, rare and expensive, with a strong earthy aroma.

Preparations

Aïoli *(ah-yoh-LEE)*
Garlic mayonnaise.

Ballotine *(bah-loh-TEEN)*, **Galantine** *(gah-lahⁿ-TEEN)*
These terms are often used interchangeably to mean some type of meat, usually chicken, stuffed, rolled, tied,

cooked, sliced, and served hot or cold. The stuffings are invariably highly seasoned forcemeats.

Barquette *(bahr-KEHT)*
Puff pastry filled with seafood, meats, or vegetables in sauces.

Beurre fondue *(buhr foh^n-DEW)*
Melted butter.

Beurre noir *(buhr NWAHR)*
Browned butter.

Bordure *(bohr-DEWR)*
Ragout of various foods.

Bouchée *(boo-SHAY)*
A puff pastry shell for holding meat or vegetable stews. Chicken à la king is an old standard for filling a bouchée.

Brochette, en Brochette *(broh-SHEHT)*
A skewer, food cooked on a skewer.

Brunoise *(brew-NWAHZ)*
Very small dice of vegetables.

Chiffonade *(shee-foh-NAHD)*
Fresh herbs cut into fine strips or ribbons.

Confit *(koh^n-FEE)*
Meat cooked and preserved in its own fat, as duck or goose. Or, preserved vegetables and/or fruits (usually in sugar, vinegar, and maybe brandy).

Consommé *(koh^n-soh-MAY)*
Clear broth.

Coulis *(koo-LEE)*
Sauce made of a purée.

Crème *(KREHM)*
Cream or cream soup.

Crêpe *(KREHP)*
French pancake (very thin), used in either sweet or savory dishes.

Crudités (krew-dee-TAY)

Raw vegetables.

Duxelles (dewk-SEHL)

Finely chopped mushrooms and shallots, sautéed, then simmered with white wine.

Fines herbes (feen-ZEHRB)

Originally, a mixture of chopped herbs, often parsley, chervil, tarragon, and chives. Often, just chopped parsley, as in *omelette fines herbes*.

Fricassée (free-kah-SAY)

A stew of white meat (chicken, veal). The meat is seared without browning, then braised.

Galantine (gah-lah^n-TEEN)

See ballotine.

Gratin (grah-TEH^N)

Covered with bread crumbs and grated cheese and then baked.

Macedoine (mahs-DWAHN)

Mixture of fruit or vegetables.

Mignardises (mee-nyahr-DEEZ)

Delicacies and dainty items. Generally referring to small sweets presented in a restaurant just before or with the check.

Mimosa (mee-moh-SAH)

Hard-boiled egg yolk garnish made by pressing the yolk through a sieve.

Mousse (MOOS)

Meat, fish, or sweets puréed with egg and cream, sometimes whipped egg whites. The word literally means "foam" or "lather," thus "something smooth."

Mousseline (moos-LEEN)

Hot preparation of meat or fish mixed with egg white and usually cream, steamed or baked to form a rather light product.

Moutarde (moo-TAHRD)

Mustard.

Pannequets (pahn-KEH)

Filled pancakes.

Pâte à choux (pah-tah SHOO)

Cream puff or *éclair* paste. May have sweet or savory filling. Small puffs made from this paste are called *profiteroles*.

Pâte brisée (paht bree-ZAY)

Basic pie dough.

Pâte millefeuilles or *pâte feuilletée (paht meel-FOY/foy-yuh-TAY)*

Puff pastry ("pastry of a thousand leaves" or "pastry leaved").

Pâté, Terrine (pah-TAY, teh-REEN)

A *terrine* is an earthenware dish in which meat and game are cooked. Also, the food itself that is cooked in the dish. Generally, chopped and puréed meats, highly seasoned. A *pâté* is, strictly speaking, baked inside a pie crust, but the term is used as a synonym for *terrine*. Don't confuse with "tureen," which is a dish for serving soup. Also, notice that *pâte* means pie dough, and *pâté* means the French meatloaf.

Quenelles (kuh-NEHL)

Fish dumplings. Often used in soups. They're better than they sound, but not a whole lot better.

Ragoût (rah-GOO)

Stew.

Rillettes (ree-YEHT)

Pork cooked in its own fat and made into a *pâté*. These days, other meats are included in the usage.

Rouille (ROO-yuh)

Sauce for bouillabaisse made from mayonnaise, garlic, and hot peppers.

Salmis (sahl-MEE)
Any dish made from game.

Tapenade (tahp-NAHD)
A spread of anchovies, black olives, garlic, olive oil, and other herbs or ingredients of choice, such as basil, tuna, or parsley. A favorite appetizer from Provence.

Herbs, Spices, Nuts, and Condiments

HERBS

Piment Rouge (pee-mah^n ROOZH)
Red pepper, the chile type.

Basilic (bah-zee-LEEK)
Basil.

Cerfeuil (sehr-FOY)
Chervil.

Ciboulette (see-boo-LEHT)
Chives.

Aneth (ah-NEHT)
Dill.

Laurier (loh-RYAY)
Bay.

Lavande (lah-VAH^{N}D)
Lavender.

Marjolaine (mahr-zho-LEHN)
Marjoram.

Menthe (MAH^{N}T)
Mint.

Origan (oh-ree-GAH^N)
Oregano.

Persil (pehr-SEE)
Parsley.

Romarin (roh-mah-REH^N)
Rosemary.

Sauge (SOHZH)
  Sage.

Sariette (sah-RYEHT)
  Savory.

Estragon (ehs-trah-GOH^N)
  Tarragon.

Thym (TEH^m)
  Thyme.

SPICES

Capres (KAH-pruh)
  Capers.

Anis (ah-NEES)
  Anise.

Cumin (kew-MEH^N)
  Cumin.

Carvi (kahr-VEE)
  Caraway.

Cannelle (kah-NEHL)
  Cinnamon.

Girofles (zhee-RUH-fluh)
  Cloves.

Fenouil (fuh-NOO-yuh)
  Fennel.

Épices (ay-PEES)
  Spices.

Fenugrec (fuh-new-GREHK)
  Fenugreek.

Gingembre (zheh^m-ZHAH^M-bruh)
  Ginger.

Genièvre (zhuh-NYEH-vruh)
  Juniper.

Moutarde (moo-TAHRD)
  Mustard.

Pavot (pah-VOH)
Poppy seeds.

Safran (sah-FRAH^N)
Saffron.

Curcuma (kewr-kew-MAH)
Turmeric.

Curry (kew-REE)
Curry.

Quatre-épices (kah-tray-PEES)
Literally, "four spices." a mixture of black peppercorns, nutmeg, cloves, and ginger. Used in charcuterie and stews.

Sel (SEHL)
Salt.

NUTS

Amandes (ah-MAH^ND)
Almonds.

Arachide (ah-rah-SHEED)
Peanuts.

Cacahouète (kah-kah-WEHT)
Peanuts.

Marrons (mah-ROH^N)
Chestnuts.

Noisettes (nwah-ZEHT)
Hazelnuts.

Noix (NWAH)
Nut or walnut.

Noix d'Acajou (NWAH dah-kah-ZHOO)
Cashew nut.

Noix de Coco (nwah duh koh-KOH)
Coconut.

Noix de pacane (nwah duh pah-KAHN)
Pecans.

Pignon (pee-NYOH^N^)
Pine nuts.

Pistaches (pee-STAHSH)
Pistachios.

CONDIMENTS

Café (kah-FEH)
Coffee.

Huile de noix (weel duh NWAH)
Walnut oil.

Huile d'olive (weel doh-LEEV)
Olive oil.

Miel (MYEHL)
Honey.

Poivre (PWAH-vruh)
Pepper, as in black, white, and green. Not related to the bell or chile peppers. See *Piment Rouge.*

Thé (TAY)
Tea.

Vinaigre (vee-NEH-gruh)
Vinegar.

Sauces

Béarnaise (bay-ahr-NEHZ)
Tarragon-flavored hollandaise.

Béchamel (bay-shah-MEHL)
Thickened milk sauce, what Mom used to call cream sauce. Used as a binder quite often in traditional French cooking.

Bercy (behr-SEE)
A butter sauce with shallots, white wine, and herbs.

Beurre blanc (buhr BLAH^N)

Very popular butter sauce that feels lighter on the palate than hollandaise. But it's mostly butter, so there's a lot of fat. Basically, whole butter emulsified in reduced wine, vinegar, and shallots. Many flavors and variations abound.

Cumberland

A cold sauce for meats made from currant jelly, port wine, and zest of orange.

Demi-glace (duh-mee GLAS)

A brown veal sauce reduced by cooking to concentrate the flavors.

Dijonnaise (dee-zhoh-NEHZ)

Mustard sauce, from Dijon mustard. Usually with cream or sour cream.

Financière (fee-nahⁿ-SYEHR)

A *demi-glace* with Madeira wine.

Hollandaise (oh-lahⁿ-DEHZ)

An emulsified butter sauce, very lemony and delicious. Served with vegetables, fish, and meats. Also used as the base for *béarnaise* (with tarragon), *choron* (sho-ROH^N, béarnaise with tomato), and *foyot* (fwah-YOH, béarnaise with beef glaze). These are a bit out of fashion as this book goes to print, because people are shying away from the egg yolks necessary to the emulsion. But these venerable sauces will endure, and without doubt they will regain their favor in the near future.

Mayonnaise (mah-yoh-NEHZ)

An emulsion of oil, vinegar, and seasonings.

Nantua (nahⁿ-tew-AH)

Purée of crayfish or lobster in white wine and cream sauce.

Ravigote (rah-vee-GUHT)

A *vinaigrette* with capers.

Remoulade (ruh-moo-LAHD)

The French version calls for mayonnaise with chopped cornichons, capers, mustard, and herbs. It's similar to tartar sauce. In New Orleans, a remoulade is pink, owing to some tomato product and spices.

Espagnole (eh-spah-NYUHL)

The traditional brown sauce of the French kitchen, generally used as a base for other brown sauces, including *demi-glace,* red wine sauces, and other pan sauces.

Madère (mah-DEHR)

Brown sauce with mushrooms and Madeira wine.

Maltaise (mahl-TEHZ)

Hollandaise with juice of the blood orange.

Suprème (sew-PREHM)

A *velouté* with cream added.

Velouté (vuh-loo-TAY)

A thickened chicken or veal stock, used as a basis for other sauces.

Dairy Products

Crème fraîche (krehm FREHSH)

A cultured product similar to sour cream, but less sour. It's between sour cream and Devonshire cream on the sour scale. *Crème fraîche* is used in French cooking rather than heavy cream. Heavy cream is used almost exclusively for whipped cream.

Crème chantilly (krehm shah[n]-tee-YEE)

Whipped cream.

Roquefort (ruhk-FORT)

Blue-veined cheese from the Roquefort region.

Lait (LEHT)

Milk.

Gruyère (grew-YEHR)

A type of Swiss cheese.

Fromage (froh-MAHZH)
Cheese.

Beurre (BUHR)
Butter.

Chèvre (SHEH-vruh)
Goat cheese. Literally, "goat."

Brie (BREEH)
Brie, a soft ripened cheese. The white rind is edible. Approximately 60 percent fat.

Camembert (kah-mah^m-BEHR)
Similar to Brie, but milder.

Doux de Montagne (doo duh moh^n-TAH-nyuh)
A cow's-milk cheese from the foot of the Pyrenees, approximately 45 percent fat. It is pale yellow with irregular holes and a mellow, sweet, nutty flavor.

Port du Salut (puhr dew sah-LEW)
A monastery cow's-milk cheese, approximately 50 percent fat. A mild cheese with an edible, bright orange rind.

Emmenthaler (eh-mah^n-tah-LEHR)
A Swiss cow's-milk cheese, approximately 45 percent fat. It is the original Swiss cheese. It is one of the basic fondue cheeses.

Morbier (mohr-BYEHR)
A firm cheese, mild, approximately 45 percent fat. A dark line runs horizontally through the cheese, the result of a layer of fat placed between the curds of the morning milk production and the curds of the evening milk production.

Boursin (boor-SEH^N)
A triple-cream cheese with 75 percent fat, usually flavored with herbs and garlic. It is a fresh cheese, creamy and mild.

Suggested Menus

Fall or Winter Bistro Menu

Soupe à l'oignon gratinée
French onion soup baked with cheese

(Beaujolais or house red, also with next course)

Poularde rôtie au jus
Roast chicken with natural juices

Salade verte
Green salad

Fromages
Cheeses

Tarte aux pommes
Apple tart

Calvados
Apple brandy

Café
Coffee

A Country Luncheon

Consommé à la Madrilène
Chilled consommé flavored with tomato

Crêpes à la Reine
Chicken crêpes

Salade Verte
Green salad

Italian

MENU GUIDE

Introduction to Italian Cuisine

WELCOME TO THE EXCITING WORLD of Italian food! The mere thought of an Italian meal evokes a relaxed sense of warmth and congeniality. Yet Italian cuisine comprises a vast variety of regional foods and dishes, and there is no Italian cuisine as such: there are many regional cuisines united primarily by a passion for excellent food. The hearty *zuppa alla marinara* (TSOO-pah AH-lah mah-ree-NAH-rah) of Naples and the elegant risottos of Milan may have little culinary history in common, but both will equally tantalize your palate.

Added to this rich variety of Italian cuisine is the American influence. Not many years ago, "Italian" food in most restaurants in the United States meant a fairly limited selection of Americanized standards. Then, in the late 1970s, a mania for "northern" Italian food began, and to a great extent it continues today. Much of that food has assumed Americanized characteristics (such as "designer" pastas, pizzas, and risottos, none of which is common in Italy). Even when the American influence is unmistakable, the basic Italian passion for making delicious food guides their production.

What especially distinguishes Italian restaurant cooking from the French is that the food you get in Italian restaurants is based on good home cooking. The primary reason for dining in Italian restaurants is therefore not to experience a new or different cuisine so much as to eat well-prepared, familiar food. This certainly carries over into Italian restaurants in the U.S., where the social aspects of the dining experience assume great importance. So, go to your nearest Italian restaurant of any style—northern, southern, American, or any other—and eat some of the best food you'll ever find in a warm, congenial atmosphere.

Buon appetito!

TYPES OF RESTAURANTS IN ITALY

Autogrill (ow-toh-GREEL)
  Roadside restaurant or snack bar.

Bar/Caffè (BAHR/kah-FEH)
  The quintessential Italian institution. Life without it would be inconceivable for an Italian. They serve coffee, tea, soft drinks, beer, liquor, and snacks such as toasts, sandwiches, and pastries. The perfect place to hang out, relax, refresh yourself, read, write, talk, watch, and be watched.

Gelateria (jeh-lah-teh-REE-ah)
  Ice cream parlor.

Locanda (loh-KAHN-dah)
  A restaurant usually located outside of the city serving simple, local food.

Osteria (oh-steh-REE-ah)
  An informal place serving simple but good food at moderate prices.

Paninoteca (pah-nee-noh-TEH-kah)
  Sandwich bar.

Ristorante (ree-stoh-RAHN-teh)
  Restaurant. The range of style, atmosphere, and price category is impressive. It's best to check the menu outside before you decide to go in.

Rosticceria (roh-stee-cheh-REE-ah)
  A place specializing mainly in grilled chicken to take out with some seating available.

Sala da tè (SAH-lah da TEH)
  "Tea room" serving tea, pastries, and in some cases light meals.

Taverna (tah-VEHR-nah)
  Eatery that lacks the refined atmosphere of a restaurant or even a trattoria. However, the food is tasty, well-prepared, and inexpensive.

Tavola calda/fredda (TAH-voh-lah KAHL-dah/FREH-dah)
  Cafeteria.

Trattoria (trah-toh-REE-ah)
  Medium-priced restaurant, often family-run, offering excellent home cooking, *cucina casalinga* (koo-CHEE-nah kah-zah-LEEN-gah).

Aperitifs

A LARGE VARIETY of Italian aperitifs *(aperitivi)* is available, even in the United States, so why don't you consider having something a little different from the usual? Italy produces several aperitifs, either wine- or spirit-based. Wine-based aperitifs are simply wines fortified with distilled spirits and often flavored with herbs and spices. Some wine-based aperitifs include marsala, vermouth, and Rosso Antica. Spirit-based aperitifs start with distilled spirits and then add flavorings. Some well-known examples are Campari, Biancosarti, and Cynar.

Wine is also commonly drunk as an aperitif. Italy is the greatest wine producer in Europe, and wine is certainly the most popular alcoholic beverage in the country. If you're unfamiliar with Italian wines, ask your server for a recommendation. A vast selection awaits your approval. Following are some suggestions for starting your meal.

PHRASES FOR ORDERING DRINKS IN ITALIAN:

liscio	*straight*
LEE-shoh	
con ghiaccio	*on the rocks*
kohn GYAH-choh	
con seltz/soda	*with soda*
kohn SEHLTS/SOH-dah	
con acqua	*with water*
kohn AHK-wah	

Americano (ah-meh-ree-KAH-noh)
An aperitif mixed from Campari and vermouth, on the rocks (with ice).

Bellini (beh-LEE-nee)
Chilled dry white wine or champagne with peach juice.

Biancosarti (byahn-koh-SAHR-tee)
With its yellow color and bittersweet flavor redolent of cinnamon and cloves, it reminds one of vermouth. Drink it chilled and neat.

Campari (kahm-PAH-ree)
A very popular spirit-based, herby bitter; best drunk with club soda and a lemon twist.

Cin-Cin (cheen-cheen)
Sweet and dry vermouth mixed, served on ice. The name comes from *Cinzano,* an Italian brand of vermouth.

Italians often say *Cin Cin!* when toasting with a drink. Another way to say "Cheers!" is *Salute!* (sah-LOO-teh), or "To your health!"

Cynar (CHEE-**nahr**)

Bittersweet, made from artichokes. They claim it makes what follows taste better, but that might be because what follows is such a relief. You decide.

Fernet Branca (fehr-NEHT BRAHN-kah)

Extremely bitter, dark-brown liqueur. Drink neat at room temperature. Also commonly drunk as a digestive.

Marsala (mahr-SAH-lah)

A fortified wine from Marsala, Sicily. The dry version makes a special aperitif. Drink it slightly chilled, neat.

Martini Cocktail (mahr-TEE-nee kohk-TEHL)

What we simply call a "martini." In Europe it's about three parts gin to one part dry vermouth, but in the United States it's mostly gin with a few drops of dry vermouth. The name may or may not come from Martini & Rossi vermouth, but it seems to preface Italian food very well. Remember the rule with martinis: one is not enough, three are too many.

Martini Bianco/Rosso (mahr-TEE-nee BYAHN-koh/ ROH-soh)

A common European way to refer to vermouth. Refers to the brand name, Martini & Rossi. You must specify sweet or dry. Order a vermouth in the United States, because when we say "martini" we mean the famous martini cocktail. The common way to drink either the sweet or dry vermouth is on the rocks with a lemon twist.

Negroni (neh-GROH-nee)

A blend of gin, sweet vermouth, and Campari served over ice. *Stia attento!* (Be careful!)

Punt e Mes (POONT eh MEHS)

Red-brown bitters with quinine, served with soda and a twist of orange.

Rosso Antico (ROH-soh ahn-TEE-koh)

A mixture of wines from Lake Garda, dark red, herby, slightly bitter. Drink it chilled and neat, with a splash of soda and a lemon twist.

Vermouth (VEHR-moot)

Comes in dry, sweet, and other designations. A fortified wine with about 18 to 20 percent alcohol, very herby. It used to include wormwood, which is "wermut" in German, and which evolved to "vermouth" in the Latin countries. The red, *rosso* (ROH-soh), is sweet, and the white, *bianco* (BYAHN-koh), is generally dry. Drink it on the rocks with a lemon twist.

Cold Appetizers and Salads

A LOT OF AMERICANS think of an *antipasto* as a plate of cold meats, relishes, salads, and other goodies. While that is one example, it's only one among hundreds. Relax and enjoy the beginning of a memorable meal.

Acciughe all'ammiraglia (ah-CHOOH-geh ahl'ah-mee-RAH-lyah)
   Fillets of anchovy in olive oil and lemon.

Acciughe alla piemontese (ah-CHOOH-geh AHL-ah pyeh-mohn-TEH-zeh)
   Anchovies marinated in olive oil and balsamic vinegar and garnished with white truffles.

Affettato misto (ah-feh-TAH-toh MEES-toh)
   A mixture of salamis.

IN THE BEGINNING:

Un tavolo per due.	A table for two.
oon TAH-voh-loh pehr DOO-eh	
Il menu, per favore.	The menu, please.
eel meh-NOO, pehr fah-VOH-reh	
La lista dei vini.	The wine list.
lah LEES-tah dey VEE-nee	
Vorrei . . .	I'd like . . .
voh-REY	

Antipasti vari (ahn-tee-PAHS-tee VAH-ree)
Assorted hors d'oeuvres, such as
pickled vegetables, olives,
sausages, fishes, cheese.
You have to ask to find
out what's included.

Antipasto alla contadina (ahn-tee-PAHS-toh AHL-ah
kohn-tah-DEE-nah)
Sliced ham and ox tongue garnished with various
pickled vegetables.

Arancino (ah-rahn CHEE-noh)
Rice ball filled with meat and cheese.

Caponata (kah-poh-NAH-tah)
Eggplant and other vegetables, olives, anchovies,
and capers with oil and vinegar. Often made with
a sweet-and-sour sauce.

Caprese (kahp-REH-zeh)
Salad made of mozzarella (probably the fresh
type), tomatoes, fresh basil, and olive oil.

> " *People love the way* mozzarella e pomodoro
> *rolls off the tongue whenever they order that par-*
> *ticular sandwich here. The funny thing is, some-*
> *times when they get what they ordered, some*
> *people will say, 'Wait a minute! I didn't order*
> *tomatoes!'* (Pomodoro *means . . . you guessed it!*)
> AMY LEE, OWNER, CONDOTTI,
> SANDWICH AND ESPRESSO BAR, NEW YORK "

Carpaccio (kahr-PAH-choh)
Raw beef, very thinly sliced. Served with various
garnishes.

Crostini alla gorgonzola (krohs-TEE-nee AHL-ah
gohr-gohn-DZOH-lah)
Crostini of polenta, with melted gorgonzola cheese.

Crostini con burro di acciughe (krohs-TEE-nee kohn BOO-roh dee ah-CHOO-geh)
　　Crostini with anchovy butter.

Gamberetti all'olio e limone (gahm-beh-REH-tee ahl'OHL-yoh eh lee-MOH-neh)
　　Shrimp marinated in olive oil and lemon.

Giardiniera (jahr-deen-YEH-rah)
　　Pickled vegetables.

Insalata di frutti di mare (een-sah-LAH-tah dee FROO-tee dee MAH-reh)
　　Seafood salad.

Prosciutto di Parma e melone (proh-SHOO-toh dee PAHR-mah eh meh-LOH-neh)
　　Prosciutto served with melon.

Sardine in saor (sahr-DEE-neh een SAH-ohr)
　　Sardines marinated in saor, a sauce of vinegar, onions, sugar, pine nuts, and raisins.

Insalata d'aragosta (een-sah-LAH-tah d'ah-rah-GOHS-tah)
　　Lobster salad.

Insalata di cetrioli (een-sah-LAH-tah dee cheh-tree-OH-lee)
　　Cucumber salad.

Insalata di frutta (een-sah-LAH-tah dee FROO-tah)
　　Fruit salad.

Insalata mista (een-sah-LAH-tah MEES-tah)
　　Mixed salad.

Insalata di pollo (een-sah-LAH-tah dee POH-loh)
　　Chicken salad.

Insalata di pomodoro (een-sah-LAH-tah dee poh-moh-DOH-roh)
　　Tomato salad.

Hot Appetizers and Vegetables

Bocconotto (boh-koh-NOH-toh)
> Chicken livers, sweetbreads, and truffles in puff pastry.

Bruschetta (broos-KEH-tah)
> Slices of toasted bread, seasoned with garlic, olive oil, and tomatoes. Many other versions are now common.

Bruschetta is one of those most mispronounced words in America. In Italian, the "ch" is pronounced as "k." Thus, the proper pronunciation is "broos-KEH-tah."

Calamari fritti (kah-lah-MAH-ree FREE-tee)
> Fried squid.

Caponata siciliana (kah-poh-NAH-tah see-cheel-YAH-nah)
> Eggplant and tomato stew.

Cipolline al dolceforte (chee-poh-LEE-neh ahl dohl-cheh-FOHR-teh)
> Sweet-and-sour pearl onions.

Finocchio con fontina (fee-NOHK-yoh kohn fohn-TEE-nah)
> Fresh fennel with fontina.

Frittata (free-TAH-tah)
> A flat omelette, but that's putting it simply. Actually, the *frittata* is as versatile as you need it to be. In the United States, you'll most often order it at

lunch. In Italy, it's usually supper. As in an omelette, just about any ingredient can be in a *frittata*. It's cooked with the ingredients stirred into it and usually flipped over, but never folded. Instead of turning it over, many people just put it in the broiler when it's time to cook the top. Some typical *frittata* ingredients include Parmesan or Swiss cheese, onions, asparagus, artichokes, fresh herbs, bell peppers, tomatoes, and zucchini. It makes a wonderful lunch that sticks to your ribs all afternoon, or a simple *frittata* can be the center of a light supper.

Funghi imbottiti (FOON-gee eem-boh-TEE-tee)
Stuffed mushrooms.

Melanzane ripiene con caciocavallo (meh-lahn-TSAH-neh ree-PYEH-neh kohn kah-choh-kah-VAH-loh)
Eggplant stuffed with cheese.

Mozzarella in carrozza (moh-tsah-REH-lah een kah-ROH-tsah)
Literally "mozzarella in a carriage." Mozzarella sandwich in crustless bread, which is dipped very briefly in milk, then floured, and finally dipped in egg and fried in oil. Despite its possible fat content, this sandwich is light and delicious. Outstanding with a dry white wine.

Pasticcetti con acciughe (pahs-tee-CHEH-tee kohn ah-CHOO-geh)
Fillets of anchovy wrapped in pastry and deep fried. It's rich and extremely satisfying.

Peperonata (peh-peh-roh-NAH-tah)
Peppers sautéed with oil and capers.

Peperoni ripieni con pane (peh-peh-ROH-nee ree-PYEH-nee kohn PAH-neh)
Peppers stuffed with bread.

Pomodori ripieni con riso
(poh-moh-DOH-ree ree-PYEH-
nee kohn REE-zoh)

    Tomatoes stuffed with rice.

Vongole oreganate (VOHN-goh-leh oh-
reh-gah-NAH-teh)

    Clams baked with oregano. These have become a
staple in American "southern" Italian restaurants,
and with good cause. Oregano goes really well
with clams.

Zucchini al forno (dzoo-KEE-nee ahl FOHR-noh)

    Baked zucchini.

Zucchini ripieni con formaggio (dzoo-KEE-nee ree-
PYEH-nee kohn fohr-MAH-joh)

    Zucchini stuffed with cheese.

I NEED . . .

Potrei avere . . .	*Could I have . . .*
poht-RAY ah-VEH-reh . . .	
un tovagliolo?	*a napkin?*
oon toh-vah-LYOH-loh?	
una forchetta?	*a fork?*
OO-nah fohr-KEH-tah?	
un coltello?	*a knife?*
oon kohl-TEH-loh?	
un cucchiaio?	*a table spoon?*
oon kook-YAH-yoh?	

Soups

Acquacotta (ahk-wah-KOH-tah)

Traditional vegetable soup from Tuscany. Although recipes vary, it's basically onions, celery, tomatoes, and garlic, often with eggs and Parmesan whipped in. The soup is served over crusty bread.

Brodo (BROH-doh)

Broth.

Cicoria, cacio e uova (chee-KOH-ryah, KAH-choh eh WOH-vah)

Chicory, pecorino, and egg soup. A nice, light brothy soup.

Fagioli con cavolo nero alla Toscana (fah-JOH-lee kohn KAH-voh-loh NEH-roh AHL-ah tohs-KAH-nah)

A classic hearty Tuscan soup with black cabbage, carrots, onion, leeks, celery, tomatoes, basil, parsley, and thyme.

Mariconda (mah-ree-KOHN-dah)

Beef broth with bread dumplings.

Maritata (mah-ree-TAH-tah)

Cabbage, escarole, and sausage soup.

Mesciua (mehs-CHOO-ah)

Soup made from chick peas, beans, and wheat.

Minestra con fiori di zucca (mee-NEHS-trah kohn FYOH-ree dee TSOO-kah)

Basic chicken broth with some diced vegetables and zucchini flowers. The zucchini flowers add a delightful bouquet to this simple soup.

Minestrone (mee-nehs-TROH-neh)

The name given to thick vegetable soup, of which there are many varieties. For some *minestroni,* the vegetables are cooked in oil, butter, or pancetta, while for others they are simply boiled in broth. It seems that the only real requirement is a thick, delicious outcome. Minestrone will contain at least three kinds of vegetables, and usually pasta and beans. If it contains a starch, it will always be seasoned with grated cheese.

Pasta e fagioli (PAHS-tah eh fah-JOH-lee)

Pasta and beans in a broth. Every region of Italy seems to have its own version of this classic soup. Usually, *borlotti* (bohr-LOH-tee) or *cannellini* (kah-neh-LEE-nee) beans are used, and the liquid may be water or broth. The pasta may be macaroni, *ditalini* (dee-tah-LEE-nee), or anything similar. Parmesan is added at the end.

Stracciatella alla romana (strah-chah-TEH-lah AHL-ah roh-MAH-nah)

Parmesan cheese and egg drop soup, usually in a beef broth.

Italian cuisine generally presents many opportunities for vegetarians. A basic pasta or risotto can form the basis of a satisfying meal. Polenta, great breads, soups, and salads are other good ideas for vegetarian dishes. As with other types of restaurants, special requests are appreciated in advance.

Pasta, Rice, Risotto, Polenta, and Dumplings

PASTASCIUTTA (PAHS-TAH-SHOO-TAH), or pasta with sauce, is the traditional Italian first course, a national treasure, a gastronomic religion. In many parts of Italy, no meal would be conceivable without it.

Pasta is made from flour and water, with eggs and oil sometimes used. The two general types are dried and fresh. Dry pasta is made from semolina—flour from the very hard durum wheat—and water. Eggs are never used in semolina pasta in Italy, but they are sometimes used in the United States. Quality is determined chiefly by the hardness of the wheat, the skill used in manufacturing, and the drying process. Many Italian-Americans refer to any dry pasta as "macaroni," although, strictly speaking, macaroni are short, hollow tubes of dry pasta.

Fresh pasta made commercially sometimes uses semolina, but homemade pasta—considered by many traditional cooks to be the only "true" fresh pasta—is always made from all-purpose flour, and usually includes oil and eggs. There is a common American misconception that pasta is not authentic unless made from semolina, but that is simply not true. Another misconception is that fresh pasta is superior to dried. They're different, but one is not better than the other. With some overlap in use, Italian cooks have fairly rigid ideas about which pasta should be used with which sauce. Dried pasta tends to be stronger and supports heavier sauces and ingredients, while fresh pasta is more suitable for the stuffed varieties.

There are seemingly innumerable shapes and sizes of pasta. What follow are some common shapes found in restaurants. Most can be either fresh or dried.

Spaghetti. The common string-like shape of the traditional spaghetti includes several types of pasta. From thinnest to thickest: *cappelli d'angelo* (kah-PEH-lee d'AHN-jeh-loh), *cappellini* (kah-peh-LEE-nee), *capelvenere* (kah-pehl-VEH-neh-reh), *vermicelli* (vehr-mee-CHEH-lee), *spaghettini* (spah-geh-TEE-nee), *spaghetti* (spah-GEH-tee).

Linguini. Long strings, flat rather than round, include, from thinnest to thickest: *linguini* (leen-GWEE-nee), *trenette* (treh-NEH-teh), *fettuccini* (feh-too-CHEE-nee), *tagliatelle* (tah-lyah-TEH-leh). Especially good with vegetable, fish, and meat sauces.

Penne, penne rigate, ziti. Short tubes, from smallest to largest, include: *ditalini* (dee-tah-LEE-nee), *ditali* (dee-TAH-lee), *maccheroni* (mah-keh-ROH-nee), *penne* (PEH-neh), *penne rigate* (PEH-neh ree-GAH-teh), ridged penne, *ziti* (TSEE-tee), *rigatoni* (ree-gah-TOH-nee), and *manicotti* (mah-nee-KOH-tee), which are often made from thin pancakes rather than pasta.

Fusilli, shells, wheels, bowties. Other short shapes include: *fusilli* (foo-ZEE-lee), which are spirals; *conchiglie* (kohn-KEE-lyeh), shells; *rotelle* (roh-TEH-leh), wheels; and *farfalle* (fahr-FAH-leh), bow ties.

Orzo. A pasta that has become especially popular in recent years even in non-Italian cuisine is *orzo* (OHR-tsoh), which resembles long-grain rice.

Ravioli, tortellini, cannelloni. Stuffed pastas include: *agnolini* (ah-nyoh-LEE-nee), stuffed rings; *cannelloni* (kah-neh-LOH-nee), large tubes; *cappelletti* (kah-peh-LEH-tee), little hats; *ravioli* (rah-vee-OH-lee), filled squares; and *tortellini* (tohr-teh-LEE-nee), hat-like rings.

Al dente means "to the tooth," or slightly chewy. It is used to describe pasta and rice. The inside should be somewhat hard and uncooked, but the overall sensation is "crisp-tender." The pronunciation is "ahl DEN-teh." Some people like to pronounce the second word as if it's the famous Italian poet of antiquity, Dante Alighieri, but that's incorrect.

Cappellini con salsa verde (kah-peh-LEE-nee kohn SAHL-sah VEHR-deh)

Cappellini with a green sauce of basil, parsley, garlic, parmesan, and olive oil.

Carrettiera (kah-reht-YEH-rah)

Spaghetti with onions, garlic, parsley, and bread crumbs.

Farfalle al pomodoro fresco (fahr-FAH-leh ahl poh-moh-DOH-roh FREHS-koh)

Pasta bowties with fresh tomato and herb sauce.

Fettuccine alfredo (feh-too-CHEE-neh ahl-FREH-doh)

Fettuccini with egg yolks, cream, and parmesan.

DID YOU KNOW?

Fettuccine Alfredo has been a classic tableside preparation for many years, and has remained so consistently popular that all sorts of "Alfredo" derivatives have sprung up throughout America. For example, restaurants have "pasta and broccoli Alfredo," "chicken and asparagus Alfredo on penne," etc. But the history of Fettuccine Alfredo, and the proper preparation of it, should not get blurred by these often inexpert variations.

Alfredo, who owned a restaurant in Rome, adapted this dish from the classic *fettuccine alla doppia crema* (fettucine with double cream). Essentially, the pasta is mixed with double cream and Parmesan, and finished with freshly ground black pepper. Fettuccine Alfredo includes egg yolks and butter, just in case the fat content of the heavy cream is inadequate!

Gnocchi alla romana (NYOH-kee AHL-ah roh-MAH-nah)

Semolina gnocchi baked with butter and parmesan.

Linguini al tonno (leen-GWEE-nee ahl TOH-noh)

Linguini with tuna sauce.

Linguini alle vongole (leen-GWEE-nee AHL-eh VOHN-goh-leh)

Linguine with clams. A simple combination that keeps on pleasing.

Risi e bisi (REE-zee eh BEE-zee)

A Venetian dish of rice and fresh peas. Despite its humble sound, the dish's combination of pancetta, butter, olive oil, onion, peas, parsley, Parmesan, and beef broth makes a tasty supper.

Riso in cagnon (REE-zoh een kah-NYOHN)
Rice with sage and parmesan. Simple and delicious.

Risotto (ree-ZOH-toh)
Rice dish typical of northern Italy using arborio rice, a round rice. The cooking method creates a creamy sauce from the surface starch and the cooking liquid (usually water, chicken broth, or veal stock), and the rice itself remains *al dente*.

Risotto alla milanese (ree-ZOH-toh AHL-ah mee-lah-NEH-zeh)
Risotto made with beef broth, saffron, and Parmesan, a specialty of Milan.

Spaghetti alla carbonara (spah-GEH-tee AHL-ah car-bo-NAH-rah)
Spaghetti with a sauce of pancetta, egg yolks, cream, and Parmesan. Literally, "in the style of the coal miner."

Spaghetti alla puttanesca (spah-GEH-tee AHL-ah poo-tah-NEHS-kah)
Spaghetti with anchovies, tomatoes, olives, garlic, capers, and hot pepper. The name literally means "in the manner of a libertine." The reason for the name remains uncertain, but the gutsy, piquant sauce may be a salute to the style of the ladies of the evening.

Pizzas, Focaccias, and Bread

THE ORIGIN OF PIZZA is uncertain, and the discussion thereof creates heated conversation. Why do people care? Because pizza is one of the most popular foods in the United States. There is a reasonable argument that the popularity of pizza in America actually led to the widespread consumption of pizza throughout northern Italy and Europe. But even that is unimportant. What is important is eating some kind of pizza on a regular basis. It's delicious!

Americans traveling to Italy are frequently disappointed by the pizza. Italian pizza, which is traditionally served in individual sizes, often includes ingredients that we don't see on pizza: ham, various unfamiliar sausages, seafoods. In Naples, the purported home of pizza, the crust is thin, and the pie is in the style most Americans find familiar, even if the toppings are unusual. But people seem to crave the pizza they grew up with. New Yorkers like a thin-crusted, cheesy pie with minimal sauce and a good quantity of olive oil, oregano, and sometimes hot pepper. Chicagoans like a deep-dish pie, filled with ingredients. Everywhere in the world, people have an opinion on what pizza should be. Perhaps the best approach is simply to enjoy whatever style you get, provided it's good. Make that the acid test. The newest American trends in pizza started with the so-called California style, inspired by Michael McCarty and Wolfgang Puck in Los Angeles. Some characteristics include a sweeter, more tender crust; a de-emphasis on tomatoes and mozzarella; and the introduction of a host of new toppings. New pizza chains recognize this taste difference and cater to it. The traditional chewy crust is undesirable to a large portion of the country.

Calzone (kahl-TSOH-neh)

Literally "trouser leg." It was originally cylindrically shaped. Now it is a crescent-shaped turnover made from pizza dough and filled with mozzarella, Parmesan, and ricotta cheeses, and typically some combination of prosciutto, tomatoes, anchovies, onions, capers, salami, or mushrooms. A specialty of Naples, *calzone* is growing in popularity because it is versatile and convenient to eat.

Carta da musica (KAHR-tah dah MOO-zee-kah)

A Sardinian bread, very thin and crusty.

Focaccia (foh-KAH-chah)

A flat bread, similar to a thick pizza, but with the texture of bread. There are all sorts of *focaccia*. A simple version is *focaccia alla Genovese* (AHL-ah jeh-noh-VEH-zeh)—just the dough and olive oil. Coarse salt, olives, tomatoes, anchovies, and Parmesan are all popular toppings. And, of course, extra-virgin olive oil. There are some sweet *focacce,* and expect more as today's chefs discover the versatility of this simple bread.

Galletta (gah-LEH-tah)
Thin biscuit (cracker).

Grissini (gree-SEE-nee)
These are the thin, dry bread sticks in cellophane wrappers. They originated in Turin and are now ubiquitous here and in Italy.

Pane (PAH-neh)
Bread. As in the rest of Europe, bread is very important to the Italian meal. In Italy restaurants often put a bread charge on the check, but we've yet to see that here. Restaurants seldom make their own bread, so the quality you get will depend on the bakeries in the local area. We hope it lives up to the rest of the meal.

Pane casareccio (PAH-neh kah-zah-REH-choh)
A large, crusty bread with tomato, mozzarella, and basil.

Pizza margherita (PEE-tsah mahr-geh-REE-tah)
With tomato, mozzarella, ham, mushrooms, and artichoke hearts.

Pizza napoletana (PEE-tsah nah-poh-leh-TAH-nah)
With tomato, mozzarella, anchovies, and oregano.

Pizza quattro stagioni (PEE-tsah KWAH-troh stah-JOH-nee)
With tomato, mozzarella, ham, sausage, mushrooms, and artichoke hearts. Divided into four quadrants (the "four seasons").

Pizza romana (PEE-tsah roh-MAH-nah)
With tomatoes, mozzarella, anchovies, capers, and oregano.

Pizza rustica (PEE-tsah ROOS-tee-kah)

> Cheeses and cured meats encased in a sweet pie dough. A specialty of Abruzzi.

Pizza siciliana (PEE-tsah see-cheel-YAH-nah)

> With tomatoes, anchovies, and pecorino cheese.

DID YOU KNOW?

The first known pizzeria opened its doors in Naples, Italy, in 1830 and remains open to this day. Gennaro Lombardi opened the first U.S. pizza shop in 1905 in New York City at 53⅓ Spring Street.

Entrées

MEAT ENTRÉES

IN ITALY, A SLICE OF MEAT, *una fettina* (OO-nah feh-TEE-nah), usually follows pasta and is ordered with a side dish, *un contorno* (oon kohn-TOHR-noh). In America, Italian restaurants tend to serve complete meals, which include both the meat and the side dish.

HOW DO YOU LIKE YOUR MEAT COOKED?

al sangue ahl SAHNG-weh	*rare*
cottura media koh-TOO-rah MEHD-yah	*medium*
ben cotta behn KOH-tah	*well-done*

Affettato (ah-feh-TAH-toh)
  A platter of sliced pork meats, served with crusty bread and butter.

Bollito misto (boh-LEE-toh MEES-toh)
  Mixed boiled meats, generally served with green sauce—*bagnet verd* (bah-NYEH VEHR) or *mostarda di frutta* (mohs-TAHR-dah dee FROO-tah). This is a classic dish, including veal breast, brisket of beef, pig's foot, calf's head, chicken, sausage, and veal tongue. The meat is presented in the broth, then carved and served with pickled vegetables. Not all the meats listed are always included.

Busecca (boo-SEH-kah)
Tripe with white beans, from Milan.

Carbonade (kahr-boh-NAH-deh)
A beef stew from Valle d'Aosta in northwestern Italy.

Cassoeula (KAH-soh-eh-oo-lah)
Various pork products braised with cabbage: ribs, sausages, etc.

Fritto misto (FREE-toh MEES-toh)
Mixed fried meats and vegetables.

Ossobuco (OH-soh BOO-koh)
Braised veal shank. The traditional *ossobuco alla milanese* generally does not include tomatoes, but rather garlic, lemon rind, parsley, and veal stock. The normal accompaniment is *risotto alla milanese* (risotto with saffron). Tomatoes are often added, much to the dismay of Milanese purist chefs, but *ossobuco* of any style is a delicious dish. Special spoons are served to dig the marrow from the bones.

Peposo (peh-POH-zoh)
Braised pork shank.

Piccata di vitello (pee-KAH-tah dee vee-TEH-loh)
Scallops of veal sautéed with butter and lemon juice. A simple and delightful way to enjoy veal.

Pollo alla cacciatora (POH-loh AHL-ah kah-chah-TOH-rah)
Chicken "hunter's style," which usually means with tomatoes, garlic, onions, mushrooms, and wine.

Salmi (SAHL-mee)
A stew of wild game.

Saltimbocca (sahl-teem-BOH-kah)
Literally: "jump in the mouth." Sautéed veal with prosciutto, sage, and white wine.

Valdostana (vahl-dohs-TAH-nah)
A veal chop stuffed with fontina cheese, breaded and sautéed.

Vitello tonnato (vee-TEH-loh toh-NAH-toh)
Veal with tuna. Served cold, the veal is sliced and coated with pureed tuna, anchovies, and capers.

SEAFOOD ENTRÉES

Brodetto (broh-DEH-toh)
A Venetian fish stew.

Burrida (boo-REE-dah)
Mediterranean catfish with a walnut sauce.

Cacciucco (kah-CHOO-koh)
Tuscan fish stew served over bread slices.

Carpione (kahr-PYOH-neh)
Fried fish with vinegar and oil.

Fritto di calamari alle erbe (FREE-toh dee kah-lah-MAH-ree AH-leh EHR-beh)
Deep-fried calamari with fresh mixed herbs.

Gamberi con burro e limone (GAHM-beh-ree kohn BOO-roh eh lee-MOH-neh)
Shrimp in butter and lemon sauce.

Grigliata di sarde alla siciliana (gree-LYAH-tah dee SAHR-deh AH-lah see-cheel-YAH-nah)
Sardines grilled and served with arugula and fennel salad.

Impepata di cozze (eem-peh-PAH-tah dee KOH-tseh)
Mussels steamed with lemon and parsley.

Polipo e patate alla ligure (POH-lee-poh eh pah-TAH-teh AH-lah lee-GOO-reh)
Octopus with boiled potatoes and haricot vert.

Shrimp *scampi*? What's the story? *Scampi* are prawns (shrimp) measuring up to several inches. Since they are often sautéed or broiled with garlic, many American restaurants feature a dish called "shrimp scampi," a redundancy in two languages. It means shrimp cooked in garlic. Scampi are simply shrimp, and *shrimply* delicious!

Salmone con insalatina estiva e pomodori essicati (sahl-MOH-neh kohn een-sah-lah-TEE-nah eh-STEE-vah eh poh-moh-DOH-ree eh-see-KAH-tee)
　　Grilled salmon served on a salad and sun-dried tomato vinaigrette.

Spigola all'acqua pazza (SPEE-goh-lah ahl-AH-kwah PAH-tsah)
　　Striped bass filet with clams, lemon, and potatoes in a light tomato broth.

Tonno in crosta di pepe nero (TOH-noh een KROH-stah dee PEH-peh NEH-roh)
　　Seared black pepper tuna.

Zuppa di pesce (TSOO-pah dee PEH-sheh)
　　Fish soup.

Zuppetta di frutti di mare (tsoo-PEH-tah dee FROO-tee dee MAH-reh)
　　Warm seafood soup in a light tomato sauce.

Desserts and Sweets

Aranciata (ah-rahn-CHAH-tah)
A Sardinian torrone, orange-flavored.

Babà (bah-BAH)
A yeast dough, soaked in syrup and flavoring. The most common is *babà al rum* with rum mixed in the syrup.

Busecchina (boo-seh-KEE-nah)
Pureed fresh chestnuts baked with cream, a Milanese specialty.

Bussola (BOO-soh-lah)
A sweet yeast bread made with liqueur, and sometimes candied fruit and nuts.

Cannoli (kah-NOH-lee)
Pastry tubes, filled with sweet ricotta cream. Yummy. An old Sicilian standard.

Cantucci (kahn-TOO-chee)
Biscuits with almonds and pine nuts.

Cassata (kah-SAH-tah)
An ice-cream cake, often with cream and custard, and multiple flavors of ice cream, a specialty of Sicily.

Castagnaccio (kah-stah-NYAH-choh)
Tuscan dessert of chestnut flour, raisins, pine nuts, and whipped cream.

Cioccolata (choh-koh-LAH-tah)
Chocolate.

Crema pasticcera (KREH-mah pahs-tee-CHEH-rah)
Pastry cream (rich vanilla pudding).

Gelato (jeh-LAH-toh)

Ice cream. But that isn't saying much. *Gelato* has to be the ice-cream lover's paradise. Italian ice creams are actually lower in butterfat content than super-premium American ice creams, but a great deal more flavoring is used. Actually, they're thin pastry cream—milk, sugar, egg yolks, and flavoring—that is frozen into ice cream. Typical flavorings are vanilla, cream, hazelnut, chocolate, and *zabaglione*. In general, in Europe and the Americas, as one travels from hotter climates to cooler climates, the ice cream becomes higher in butterfat and less intense in flavor. Go figure.

Granita (grah-NEE-tah)

A sort of sorbet (water ice) made from fruit juice and syrup, frozen and then shaved. Also made from coffee.

Marzapane (mahr-tsah-PAH-neh)

Almond paste made by pureeing almonds and sugar.

Millefoglie (mee-leh-FOH-lyeh)

Literally "a thousand leaves." Layers of crisp, light, buttery pastry dough.

Pandolce (pahn-DOHL-cheh)

Sweet bread that is packed with candied fruit.

Semifreddo (seh-mee-FREH-doh)

Frozen creams made from custard and whipped cream.

Spumone (spoo-MOH-neh)

See *Semifreddo*.

Tiramisù (tee-rah-mee-SOO)

Literally, "pull me to you." Sponge cake or ladyfingers soaked in brandy and espresso, layered with a mascarpone and egg cream, flavored with chocolate.

Torrone (toh-ROH-neh)

Candy made of sugar, honey, hazelnuts, and almonds. There are very thin wafers on the top and bottom of the sugar mixture.

Zabaglione (dzah-bah-LYOH-neh)

A custard of egg yolks cooked with Marsala and sugar, whipped continuously until fluffy. It is usually served either warm or chilled with fruit.

Zuccotto (tsoo-KOH-toh)

Round sponge cake with chocolate, cream, and candied fruit; best if chilled.

Zuppa Inglese (TSOO-pah een-GLEH-zeh)

Literally, "English soup." There are different styles, but generally it is pound cake soaked in liqueurs and layered with pastry cream. In southern versions there is meringue on top, but in other areas pastry cream is used. A definite must if you've never tried it.

Wines and After-Dinner Drinks

WINES

WINE IS THE ITALIAN national drink. The general rule applies: white wine with fish, chicken, and egg dishes, and red wine with dark meats. The availability of Italian wines in the United States has increased enormously. Outstanding wines are now easy to find, many at very good values. Below are just a few well-known types. Be sure to ask the server for suggestions. There is a huge cellar waiting for your selection.

> " *At one of my dinner parties I was asked why European people, especially Italians, always drink wine with their meals, and I found myself quoting Dante Alighieri:* 'Un pranzo senza vino è come un giorno senza sole.' *(A meal without wine is like a day without sunshine.)*
> VINCENT VIGLIOTTI, CEC, EXECUTIVE CHEF, RISTORANTE DEGREZIA, NEW YORK "

Amarone (ah-mah-ROH-neh)
 A big red wine, high alcohol content, and expensive.

Barbaresco (bahr-bah-REHS-koh)
 A softer, less intense red wine from the same grapes as *Barolo (nebbiolo)*.

Bardolino (bahr-doh-LEE-noh)
 A light red wine from the Corvina Veronese grape, much like *Valpolicella*.

Barolo (bah-ROH-loh)

A big, velvety red wine from Piedmont; one of Italy's most famous wines.

Brunello di Montalcino (broo-NEH-loh dee mohn-tahl-CHEE-noh)

One of the great red wines of the world, made from the Brunello grape. Choose the oldest you can afford; this wine needs a lot of time.

Chianti (KYAHN-tee)

A common red wine from Tuscany, made primarily from the Sangiovese grape. The best is *Chianti Classico*.

Frascati (frahs-KAH-tee)

A light-bodied white wine.

Lambrusco (lahm-BROOS-koh)

A semi-dry red wine from Emilia Romagna; lively, light, and fun.

Pinot Grigio (PEE-noh GREE-joh)

A white wine variety from the northeastern areas of Italy; light yellow to golden, generally dry, light-bodied, and lively.

Soave (SWAH-veh)

A light-bodied white wine.

Valpolicella (vahl-poh-lee-CHEH-lah)

A light red wine from the north, made from the Corvina Veronese grape.

AFTER-DINNER DRINKS

Italy has a large selection of after-dinner drinks from which to choose. They range from very sweet to very dry and from high alcohol content to low. The Italian passion for great taste that leads to such wonderful foods also produces wonderful spirits. But be careful; they're meant to be consumed in moderation!

Alchermes (ahl-KEHR-mehs)

A red liqueur, delicately scented, used in *zuppa inglese*.

Amaretto di Saronno (ah-moh-REH-toh dee sah-ROH-noh)

A liqueur flavored with ground apricot pits; sweet, with an almond flavor.

Anisetta (ah-nee-SEHT-ah)

A licorice-flavored liqueur, drunk with coffee. In many old-time Italian-American restaurants, the waiter placed a bottle on the table when coffee was served.

Averna (ah-VEHR-nah)

A bitter digestive, developed by the monks of Santo Spirito Abbey in Sicily. The recipe is secret. The taste is of cola and vanilla, bittersweet. Served at room temperature and neat.

Brandy

Unlike France, Italy has no tradition of obsession for fine brandies like those found in the Cognac and Armagnac regions. Instead, they produce good, solid, unpretentious brandies that satisfy the appetite without the fussiness. The most famous and most available Italian brandy is Stock 84, a very good choice.

Fernet Branca (fehr-NEHT BRAHN-kah)

Extremely herby, dark, bitter. Reminds some people of medicine, others sip it with delight. Drink it neat, at room temperature.

Frangelico (frahn-JEH-lee-koh)
Hazelnut liqueur.

Galliano (gah-lee-AH-noh)
A yellow, vanilla- and licorice-
flavored liqueur.

Grappa (GRAH-pah)
A distilled beverage made from the pomace, the
skin, pulp, and seeds left over from wine making.
Essentially, *grappa* is a brandy. Most are drunk
clear, unaged, but there are several aged varieties
as well. Perfect on a cold day in Venice.

Marsala (mahr-SAH-lah)
A fortified wine from Marsala, Sicily. The sweet
version makes a good after-dinner drink, and is a
key ingredient in *zabaglione*.

Opal e Nera (OH-pahl eh NEH-rah)
Licorice-flavored, like Sambuca, but dark.

Sambuca (sahm-BOO-kah)
Like anisette, but with a much higher alcohol
content.

Strega (STREH-gah)
Yellow, with a taste of herbs and spices.

CHECK, PLEASE!

Il conto, per favore.	*The check, please.*
eel KOHN-toh, pehr fah-VOH-reh.	
C'è un errore.	*There's a mistake.*
CHEH oon eh-ROH-reh.	
Tutto è stato ottimo.	*Everything was great.*
TOO-toh eh STAH-toh OH-tee-moh.	
Tenga pure il resto.	*Keep the change.*
TEHN-gah POO-reh eel REHS-toh.	

Coffee

ITALIAN COFFEE is *espresso* (ehs-PREH-soh), black and strong. Most Italian restaurants here will give you American coffee unless you order *espresso,* but in Italy *un caffè* (oon kah-FEH) will get you an *espresso.* Specialty coffees, such as *caffè latte* and *cappuccino,* are usually available if there is an espresso machine.

Espresso (ehs-PREH-soh)
A thick, black coffee made by forcing water under pressure through packed, dark-roasted coffee. A *ristretto* (rees-TREH-toh) is an espresso made with only a small amount of water,

which makes the beverage very strong indeed. A *corto* (KOHR-toh) has a bit more water put through it, and a *lungo* (LOON-goh) is made with extra water, making the coffee somewhat weaker.

Caffè con panna (kah-FEH kohn PAH-nah)
Espresso with whipped cream.

Caffè latte (kah-FEH LAH-teh)
Espresso with steamed milk.

? DID YOU KNOW?
In Italy, those milky concoctions—*cappuccino* and *caffè latte*—are drunk only at breakfast, but American restaurants serve them all day. The current lingo that originated in Seattle (tall, short; single, double; etc.) thankfully hasn't hit most Italian restaurants yet. Why don't you just have *espresso* (not decaf, please!) and enjoy an authentic experience? Who needs sleep, anyway?

Cappuccino (kah-poo-CHEE-noh)
Espresso served in a large glass with steamed milk froth on top. Often topped with cinnamon, cocoa powder, shaved chocolate, or granulated sugar.

Corretto (koh-REH-toh)
Espresso with liqueur in it.

Macchiato (mahk-YAH-toh)
Espresso with a dollop of steamed milk froth.

Moca (MOH-kah)
Coffee made on the stove in a special pot used throughout Italy. It's what we call an Italian coffee pot in the United States. The water is forced up through the ground coffee and stays in the top of the pot. It is the home version of *espresso*.

TIPPING

Italians add a 10 to 15 percent service charge to the restaurant bill. If the food and service are excellent, it's always nice to give your waiter a little extra, and many will even expect it. For better and quicker service at the counter, include a small tip with your receipt.

Glossary of Ingredients and Techniques

Meats

Abbacchio (ah-BAH-kyoh)
  Baby lamb.

Agnello (ah-NYEH-loh)
  Lamb.

Anatra (ah-NAH-trah)
  Duck.

Animelle (ah-nee-MEH-leh)
  Sweetbreads (thymus gland of the calf).

Arrosto (ah-ROHS-toh)
  Roast.

Bistecca (bees-TEH-kah)
  Beef steak.

Braciola (brah-CHOH-lah)
  A pork or lamb chop or steak.

Bresaola (breh-zah-OH-lah)
  Cured beef, used in antipasto.

Cacciagione (kah-chah-JOH-neh)
  Game.

Cacciatorino (kah-chah-toh-REE-noh)
  A small salami made from pork and beef.

Cappone (kah-POH-neh)
  Capon, a castrated male chicken.

Cervello (chehr-VEH-loh)
  Brain.

Cervo (CHEHR-voh)
  Deer.

Coniglio (koh-NEE-lyoh)
  Rabbit.

Coppa (KOH-pah)
  Neck.

Costoletta *(koh-stoh-LEH-tah)*
Rib.

Cotoletta *(koh-toh-LEH-tah)*
Cutlet.

Fagiano *(fah-JAH-noh)*
Pheasant.

Fegato *(FEH-gah-toh)*
Liver.

Filetto *(fee-LEH-toh)*
Fillet.

Lardo *(LAHR-doh)*
Fat back (pork).

Lepre *(LEH-preh)*
Hare.

Lingua *(LEEN-gwah)*
Tongue.

Lombata *(lohm-BAH-tah)*
Loin.

Medaglioni *(meh-dah-LYOH-nee)*
Round tenderloin medallions.

Midollo *(mee-DOH-loh)*
Marrow.

Mocetta *(moh-CHEH-tah)*
Salami from the Valle d'Aosta,
made with venison.

Mortadella *(mohr-tah-DEH-lah)*
A sausage with chunks of fat and whole peppercorns in it,
served as a cold cut.

Nodini *(noh-DEE-nee)*
Veal chops.

Oca *(OH-kah)*
Goose.

Pancetta (pahn-CHEH-tah)
Belly of the pork, the same cut as bacon, cured and dried, but not smoked.

Pernice (pehr-NEE-cheh)
Partridge.

Pollo (POH-loh)
Chicken.

Polpetta (pohl-PEH-tah)
Meatball.

Polpettone (pohl-peh-TOH-neh)
Meat loaf.

Porchetta (pohr-KEH-tah)
Suckling pig.

Prosciutto (proh-SHOO-toh)
Parma ham.

Punta di petto (POON-tah dee PEH-toh)
Brisket of beef.

Quaglia (KWAH-lyah)
Quail.

Rognoni (roh-NYOH-nee)
Kidneys.

Rosbif (ROHZ-beef)
Roast beef.

Salame (sah-LAH-meh)
Salami (ground meat and seasonings in a casing).

Salsiccia (sahl-SEE-chah)
Sausage.

Scaloppine (skah-loh-PEE-neh)
Veal cutlets; thin slices of meat.

Selvaggina (sehl-vah-JEE-nah)
Venison.

Tacchino (tah-KEE-noh)
Turkey.

Trippa (TREE-pah)
Tripe.

Seafood

Acciughe *(ah-CHOO-geh)*
Anchovies.

Anguilla *(ahn-GWEE-lah)*
Eel.

Aragosta *(ar-rah-GOH-stah)*
Lobster.

Arringa *(ah-REEN-gah)*
Herring.

Arselle *(ahr-SEH-leh)*
Scallops.

Baccalà *(bah-kah-LAH)*
Salt cod, commonly cooked in milk after several days of soaking in many changes of water.

Branzino *(brahn-DZEE-noh)*
Bass.

Bottarga *(boh-TAHR-gah)*
The dried ovary sac of tuna or mullet, sliced as an antipasto or used for flavoring sauces.

Calamari *(kah-lah-MAH-ree)*
Squid.

Carpa *(KAHR-pah)*
Carp.

Cernia *(CHER-nee-ah)*
Grouper.

Cozze *(KOH-tseh)*
Mussels.

Frutti di mare *(FROO-tee dee MAH-reh)*
Seafood (literally, "fruits of the sea"). Shellfish only.

Gamberi *(GAHM-beh-ree)*
Shrimp.

Granchi *(GRAHN-kee)*
Crabs.

Luccio (LOO-choh)
 Pike.

Lumache di mare (loo-MAH-keh dee MAH-reh)
 Sea snails.

Merluzzo (mehr-LOO-tsoh)
 Cod.

Ostriche (ohs-TREE-keh)
 Oysters.

Pesce (PEH-sheh)
 Fish.

Pesce spada (PEH-sheh SPAH-dah)
 Swordfish.

Polipo (POH-lee-poh)
 Octopus.

Ricci (REE-chee)
 Sea urchins.

Rombo (ROHM-boh)
 Turbo.

Salmone (sahl-MOH-neh)
 Salmon.

Sardine (sahr-DEE-neh)
 Sardines.

Scampi (SKAHM-pee)
 Prawns.

Seppia (SEHP-yah)
 Cuttlefish.

Sgombro (SGOHM-broh)
 Mackerel.

Sogliola (SOH-lyoh-lah)
 Sole.

Spigola (SPEE-goh-lah)
 Sea bass.

Storione (stohr-YOH-neh)
 Sturgeon.

Tonno (TOHN-noh)
Tuna.

Triglia (TREE-lyah)
Red mullet.

Trota (TROH-tah)
Trout.

Ventaglio (vehn-TAH-lyoh)
Scallop.

Vongole (VOHN-goh-leh)
Clams.

Vegetables and Fruits

Albicoca (ahl-bee-KOH-kah)
Apricot.

Aglio (AH-lyoh)
Garlic.

Ananas (AH-nah-nahs)
Pineapple.

Anguria (ahn-GOO-ryah)
Watermelon.

Arancia (ah-RAHN-chah)
Orange.

Asparaghi (ahs-PAH-rah-gee)
Asparagus.

Barbabietola (bahr-bah-BYEH-toh-lah)
Beet.

Bianchi di spagnoni (BYAHN-kee dee spah-NYOH-nee)
White beans.

Borlotti (bohr-LOH-tee)
Medium-sized dried beans, speckled brown.

Broccoletti di rapa (broh-koh-LEH-tee dee RAH-peh)
A bitter winter green broccoli.

Broccoli (BROH-koh-lee)
Broccoli.

Cannellini (kah-neh-LEE-nee)
Small white beans.

Carciofi (kahr-CHOH-fee)
Artichokes.

Carota (kah-ROH-tah)
Carrot.

Cavolfiori (kah-vohl-FYOH-ree)
Cauliflower.

Cavoli di Brusselle (KAH-voh-lee dee broo-SEHL-eh)
Brussels sprouts.

Cavolo (KAH-voh-loh)
Cabbage.

Ceci (CHEH-chee)
Chick peas, or garbanzos.

Cedro (CHEHD-roh)
Lime.

Cicoria (chee-KOH-ryah)
Chicory (curly endive).

Ciliegie (chee-LYEH-jeh)
Cherries.

Cipolla (chee-POH-lah)
Onion.

Datteri (DAH-teh-ree)
Dates

Fagioli (fah-JOH-lee)
Beans.

Fagiolini (fah-joh-LEE-nee)
String beans.

Fichi (FEE-kee)
Figs.

Fichi secchi (FEE-kee SEH-kee
Dried figs.

Fichi d'India (FEE-kee d'EEN-dee-ah)
Prickly pears.

Finocchio (fee-NOHK-yoh)
Fennel. Often eaten raw after a meal as a sort of digestive.

Fragola (FRAH-goh-lah)
Strawberry.

Funghi (FOON-gee)
Mushrooms.

Granoturco (grah-noh-TOOR-koh)
Corn.

Indivia (een-DEE-vee-ah)
Endive.

Lampone (lahm-POH-neh)
Raspberry.

Lattuga (lah-TOO-gah)
Lettuce.

Lenticchie (lehn-TEEK-yeh)
Lentils.

Limone (lee-MOH-neh)
Lemon.

Mais (MAH-ees)
Corn.

Mandarino (mahn-dah-REE-noh)
Tangerine.

Melanzane (meh-lahn-DZAH-neh)
Eggplant.

Mela (MEH-lah)
Apple.

Melone (meh-LOH-neh)
Melon.

Mirtillo (meer-TEE-loh)
Blueberry.

Mora (MOH-rah)
Blackberry.

Patata (pah-TAH-tah)
Potato.

Peperoncino *(peh-peh-rohn-CHEE-noh)*
  Chili pepper.

Peperoni *(peh-peh-ROH-nee)*
  Bell peppers.

Pera *(PEH-rah)*
  Pear.

Pesca *(PEHS-kah)*
  Peach.

Pomo *(POH-moh)*
  Apple.

Pomodoro *(poh-moh-DOH-roh)*
  Tomato.

Pompelmo *(pohm-PEHL-moh)*
  Grapefruit.

Porcini *(pohr-CHEE-nee)*
  Wild mushrooms, called *cèpes* in France. Very flavorful, wonderful in risotto.

Porro *(POH-roh)*
  Leek.

Prugna *(PROO-nyah)*
  Plum or prune.

Radicchio *(rah-DEE-kee-yoh)*
  A red leafy vegetable, rather bitter, used in salads.

Ravanelli *(rah-vah-NEH-lee)*
  Radishes.

Sedano *(SEH-dah-noh)*
  Celery.

Spinaci *(spee-NAH-chee)*
  Spinach.

Susina *(soo-SEE-nah)*
  Plum.

Taccola *(TAK-koh-lah)*
  Snow pea.

Tartufo *(tahr-TOO-foh)*
White truffle, much more aromatic and
flavorful than the black truffle.

Uva *(OO-vah)*
Grape.

Uvetta *(oo-VEH-tah)*
Raisin.

Zucca *(TZOO-kah)*
Pumpkin.

Zucchini *(tsoo-KEE-nee)*
Italian squash.

Dairy Products

Formaggio *(fohr-MAH-joh)*
Cheese.

Asiago *(ahs-YAH-goh)*
A hard, aromatic grating cheese.

Bel Paese *(behl pah-EH-zeh)*
A soft, mild cheese.

Burro *(BOO-roh)*
Butter.

Caciocavallo *(kah-choh-kah-VAH-loh)*
A dense, mild cow's cheese from southern Italy.

Carnia *(KAHR-nyah)*
Soft, yellow cheese with a sharp taste.

Crescenza *(kreh-SHEHN-tsah)*
A fresh, buttery cheese made from cow's milk.

Fontina *(fohn-TEE-nah)*
A mild cheese from Valle d'Aosta.

Gorgonzola *(gohr-gohn-DZOH-lah)*
Flavored, pungent, creamy, white cheese with green
mold; like blue cheese, but creamier and softer.

Grana padano *(GRAH-nah pah-DAH-noh)*
See *Parmigiano-Reggiano.*

Latte (*LAH-teh*)
Milk.

Lattemiele (*lah-teh-MYEH-leh*)
Whipped cream, sweetened.

Mascarpone (*mahs-kahr-POH-neh*)
Very rich, with a texture similar to cream cheese.

Mozzarella (*moh-tsah-REH-lah*)
A mild, fresh cheese.

Parmigiano-Reggiano (*pahr-mee-JAH-noh reh-JAH-noh*)
A grating cheese made from cow's milk. Often aged two
years, sometimes longer. In the United States we call
cheeses "parmesan" if they are in the
same style, but only the authentic
Italian product can be called *Parmigiano-Reggiano*. It's worth the price
difference. Authentic *Parmigiano-Reggiano* has a deep, nutty taste that avoids the
strong smell of spoiled milk sometimes found in the
cheap imitations.

Pecorino (*peh-koh-REE-noh*)
A grating cheese made from sheep's milk, very aromatic,
often mixed with Parmesan. Many consider the *Pecorino
Romano* from Lazio to be the finest.

Provolone (*proh-voh-LOH-neh*)
A mild cheese made from cow's milk, similar to mozzarella but firmer. Sometimes aged a bit, which makes it
crumbly.

Ricotta (*ree-KOH-tah*)
A fresh cheese that resembles very small-curd cottage
cheese, but drier.

Robbiola (*roh-BYOH-lah*)
Soft, unripened cheese made from cow's milk.

Stracchino (*strah-KEE-noh*)
Soft, creamy, off-white cheese, excellent with fried polenta.

Uova (*WOH-vah*)
Eggs.

Herbs, Spices, Nuts, and Condiments

Aceto (ah-CHEH-toh)
Vinegar.

Aceto balsamico (ah-CHEH-toh bahl-SAH-mee-koh)
Balsamic vinegar.

Anice (ah-NEE-cheh)
Anise.

Bagna calda (BAH-nyah KAHL-dah)
Literally "a hot bath." A dip of
anchovies and garlic in oil.

Basilico (bah-ZEE-lee-koh)
Basil.

Buccia di frutta candita (BOO-chah dee FROO-tah kahn-DEE-tah)
Candied fruit and peel.

Cannella (kah-NEH-lah)
Cinnamon.

Balsamic vinegars have become extremely popular in recent years, and with good reason. True balsamic vinegar is made from red wine vinegar aged in a succession of wooden barrels from various woods. The aging mellows and sweetens the vinegar, covering up the acidity. The standard commercial varieties in common use are made by a quick caramelization and flavoring process, but they work very well with all sorts of salads and in meat and seafood marinades. Balsamic vinegars lack the sharpness of straight vinegars.

Some balsamic vinegars are aged for up to fifty years, which adds considerably to their cost. Those expensive varieties should be saved for special uses, such as lightly drizzling on fruits or chilled, cooked meats.

Capperi (KAH-peh-ree)
Capers, the pickled buds of a Mediterranean nasturtium shrub, very pungent.

Castagne (kahs-TAH-nyeh)
Chestnuts. Italy is second only to Japan in chestnut consumption.

Conserva di pomodori (kohn-SEHR-vah dee poh-moh-DOH-ree)
Dried and pureed tomatoes, a very concentrated preparation.

Dragoncello (drah-gohn-CHEH-loh)
Tarragon.

Lauro (LAH-oo-roh)
Bay leaf.

Maggiorana (mah-joh-RAH-nah)
Marjoram.

Mandorle (MAHN-dohr-leh)
Almonds.

Mostarda di frutta (mohs-TAHR-dah dee FROO-tah)
Fruit preserved in syrup and mustard oil, used with *bollito misto* or other boiled meat dishes. A wonderful contrast of sweet and piquant flavors, it serves much the same taste purpose as chutney with Indian curries.

Nocciola (noh-CHOH-lah)
Hazelnut.

Noccioline (noh-choh-LEE-neh)
Peanuts.

Noce (NOH-cheh)
Nut.

Noce moscata (NOH-cheh mohs-KAH-tah)
Nutmeg.

Olio d'oliva (OHL-yoh d'oh-LEE-vah)
Olive oil.

Origano (oh-REE-gah-noh)
Oregano.

Olive oil is the magic elixir of the Mediterranean, only recently gaining its rightful fame in the United States. It is currently considered very healthful and beneficial in maintaining low blood cholesterol. Extra-virgin is the finest and fruitiest, and the most expensive, with many flavor subtleties. Try extra-virgin olive oils from different countries for a taste treat. It is generally used as a condiment or in dressings, prized for its wonderful flavor. Because the smoke point of virgin olive oil is quite low, cooking is usually done in pure olive oil, which has been heat processed and has a higher smoke point. Cheapest of all is pomace olive oil, made from the last remaining olive bits after two or more pressings. It has the least aroma, but it's economical and has the highest smoke point.

Pepe nero (PEH-peh NEH-roh)
Black pepper.

Peperoncino appena macinato (peh-peh-rohn-CHEE-noh ah-PEH-nah mah-chee-NAH-toh)
Red pepper flakes (hot).

Pepolino (peh-poh-LEE-noh)
Thyme.

Pignoli (pee-NYOH-lee)
Pine nuts

Potacchio (poh-TAHK-yoh)
Foods stewed with herbs, peppers, and wine.

Prezzemolo (preh-TSEH-moh-loh)
Parsley.

Rosmarino (rohz-mah-REE-noh)
Rosemary.

Sale (SAH-leh)
Salt.

Salvia (SAHL-vyah)
  Sage.

Semi di finocchio (SEH-mee dee fee-NOHK-yoh)
  Fennel seeds.

Sesami (SEH-sah-mee)
  Sesame seeds.

Strutto (STROO-toh)
  Lard.

Cooking Terms and Techniques

Abbrustolito (ah-broo-stoh-LEE-toh)
  Grilled over an open flame.

Affogato (ah-foh-GAH-toh)
  Poached.

Affumicato (ah-foo-mee-KAH-toh)
  Smoked.

Ai ferri (ay FEH-ree)
  Grilled or barbecued.

Al dente (ahl DEHN-teh)
  Literally, "to the bite or tooth," or slightly chewy. Used for pasta and rice. The inside should be somewhat hard and uncooked, but the overall sensation is "crisp-tender."

Al forno (ahl FOHR-noh)
  Baked.

Al telefono (ahl teh-LEH-foh-noh)
  Literally, "on the telephone." The description of fritters with cheese, which form long "telephone" cords when bitten into.

Al vapore (ahl vah-POH-reh)
  Steamed.

All'onda (ahl'OHN-dah)
  Literally, "wavy." The description used for creamy risotto.

Alla bava (AH-lah BAH-vah)
  The term for cheese melted inside a dish, forming long strings.

Alla graticola (AH-lah grah-TEE-koh-lah)
  Broiled (seafood).

Alla griglia (AH-lah GREE-lyah)
  Grilled.

Allo spiedo (AH-loh SPYEH-doh)
  Broiled on a spit.

Arrosto (ah-ROHS-toh)
  Roasted.

Bollito (boh-LEE-toh)
  Boiled.

Brasato (brah-ZAH-toh)
  Braised.

Farcito (fahr-CHEE-toh)
  Stuffed.

Fritto (FREE-toh)
  Fried.

Imbottito (eem-boh-TEE-toh)
  Stuffed.

In umido (een OO-mee-doh)
  Stewed.

Lesso (LEH-soh)
  Boiled.

Marinato (mah-ree-NAH-toh)
  Marinated.

Saltato (sahl-TAH-toh)
  Sautéed.

Grain-based Foods

Ancino (ahn-CHEE-noh)
  Hard, somewhat sweet biscuits.

Crespelle (krehs-PEH-leh)
  Italian crêpes.

Crostini (krohs-TEE-nee)
  Small pieces of bread toasted, fried, or baked with oil, sometimes with cheese.

Farinacei (fah-ree-NAH-cheh-ee)

Farinaceous foods—those made from flour, such as pasta, noodles, and dumplings.

Gnocchi (NYOH-kee)

Dumplings, generally made from potatoes, but also from semolina, flour, and bread crumbs. Other ingredients and flavorings may be added. The dough resembles a wet pasta dough, or perhaps a very stiff batter. Appropriately shaped pieces are dropped into boiling water and cooked, then mixed with whatever is accompanying them. *Gnocchi* are often tossed with a small amount of tomato sauce and grated cheese, or mixed with cream sauce, or simply tossed with oil and herbs. The number of possibilities is endless. If you've never eaten them, you're in for a treat, both flavor- and texture-wise.

In cagnone (een kah-NYOH-neh)

Boiled rice served with butter and Parmesan cheese.

Mantecato (mahn-teh-KAH-toh)

A rice or pasta dish with butter and cheese.

Polenta (poh-LEHN-tah)

Cornmeal. Also the name given to the preparation of the meal into a dense mush, which is generally sliced and used in various dishes. Polenta has become extremely popular in the United States recently. Basic polenta hasn't much flavor, but rather readily takes on the flavors of other dishes, thus making a good accompaniment to stews and soups. Also, grilling or baking the polenta, and adding cheese or vegetables to the polenta, add great flavors.

Semolina (seh-moh-LEE-nah)

Semolina, the flour from durum wheat, is used to make pasta commercially. Home cooks generally use all-purpose flour.

Sauces

Agrodolce (AHG-roh-DOHL-cheh)

Sweet-and-sour sauce.

Bagnet verd (BAH-nyeh VEHR)

A sauce made from parsley, anchovies, bread, and garlic, used for boiled meats.

Besciamella (beh-shah-MEH-lah)

Béchamel (white sauce made from milk).

Concia (KOHN-chah)

A marinade. Also, a type of polenta with fontina cheese.

Fonduta (fohn-DOO-tah)

A sauce of fontina cheese and white truffles, served with polenta or crostini.

Pesto (PEHS-toh)

A pureed blend of basil, olive oil, Parmesan and/or pecorino, and pine nuts. Many variations exist, and many of today's chefs have their own signature version.

Soffritto (soh-FREE-toh)

The basis of stews, soups, sauces, and risotto. Made from cooked chopped vegetables, herbs, and spices cooked in fat until they lose their crunchiness. For example, onions sautéed in butter would be the *soffritto* for onion soup.

Typical Pasta Sauces

Agliata (ah-LYAH-tah)

A creamy garlic, bread, and oil sauce.

Alla pizzaiola (AH-lah pee-tsah-YOH-lah)

Made with tomatoes, capers, oregano, and anchovies.

Aglio, olio e peperoncino (AH-lyoh, OH-lyoh e peh-peh-rohn-CHEE-noh)

Garlic, olive oil, and dried red pepper.

Amatriciana (ah-maht-ree-CHAH-nah)

A spicy tomato-based spaghetti sauce containing hot pepper, pork, and white wine.

Bolognese (boh-loh-NYEH-zeh)

Thick meat sauce.

Carbonara (kahr-boh-NAH-rah)

Sauce used with linguine or spaghetti; made from bacon or pancetta, egg yolks, cream, and Parmesan.

Carrettiera (kah-reh-TYEH-rah)

Tomato paste, tuna, and mushrooms.

Marinara (mah-ree-NAH-rah)

Tomatoes, onion, garlic, and basil.

Puttanesca (poo-tah-NEHS-kah)

Spicy sauce of tomatoes, capers, olives, anchovies, and hot pepper.

Suggested Menus

~~~

Traditional Roman Dinner Menu

Aperitif: Campari and Soda

Stracciatella alla romana
Egg and cheese soup

(light-bodied white wine, such as a Frascati, to
accompany spaghetti as well)

Spaghetti con vongole
Spaghetti with clams

Saltimbocca alla romana
Veal sautéed with prosciutto and sage in butter and
white wine.

(light-bodied red, such as Valpolicella)

Baba al rhum
Rum-soaked yeast cake

Sambuca

Caffè
Coffee

Milanese Dinner Menu

Zuppa pavese
Chicken broth on poached eggs and crusty bread

(Pinot Grigio, also for risotto)

Risotto milanese
Creamy rice with saffron and Parmesan cheese

Ossobuco
Braised veal shank

(Barolo)

Macedonia di frutti
Fruit salad

Amaretto di Saronno

Caffè
Coffee

Traditional Tuscan Dinner Menu

Aperitif: Rabarbaro
Rhubarb-flavored aperitif

Zuppa di fagioli alla toscana
Tuscan-style bean soup

Costata alla fiorentina
Beef steak with spinach

Insalata di stagione
Mixed seasonal greens

Tartufo
Truffle-shaped dessert of ice cream covered
with chocolate

Espresso

Digestivo
After-dinner drink

Spanish
& Latin American
MENU GUIDE

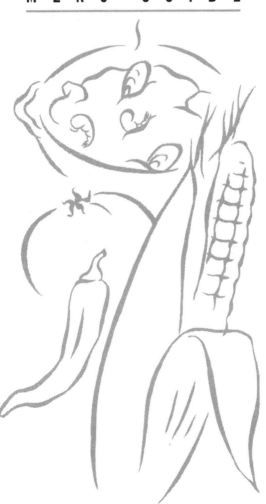

Introduction to Spanish and Latin American Cuisine

IT IS OFTEN SAID that cuisine is culture, and to understand the development of Spanish and Latin American cuisine it is important to understand something of the history of these two historically and culturally linked regions. The accidents of history have all played a part in the culinary development of these regions, from the seven and a half centuries of Moorish presence in Spain, to the Spanish colonization of the Americas. You'll find many similarities between the continents, but you will also encounter vast differences. Ultimately, dining well is an integral part of both the Latin American and Spanish lifestyles, and the joys of mealtime shine through in their vast array of dishes.

ARGENTINA

Argentine cuisine is marked by the influence of its diverse immigrant population. In the larger cities you'll find everything from Jewish delis to Italian, Spanish, and German restaurants. Since the Argentine economy is based largely on raising livestock, you'll find many beef dishes on Argentine menus. The *parrillada* (pah-ree-YAH-dah), or barbecue, is the most traditional Argentine cuisine, and *bife* (BEE-feh), beef, is its primary ingredient. It is not unusual to be served a 3-inch-thick steak along with barbecued chicken, ribs, and blood sausage with the indispensable *chimichurri* (chee-mee-CHOO-rree) sauce made with olive oil, vinegar, garlic, and cilantro. *Milanesas* (mee-lah-NEH-sahs), breaded beef or chicken cutlets, and *empanadas* (ehm-pah-NAH-dahs), pastries stuffed with ground beef, are also popular Argentine dishes.

BRAZIL

Brazilian cuisine is rich in variety and tradition. Many of its traditional dishes are adaptations of Portuguese specialties. Beef stews called *cozidos* (koh-ZEE-dohs) and fish stews called *caldeiras* (kahl-DAY-rahs) are examples of the strong Portuguese influence. *Camarão bahiana* (kah-mah-RAW bah-EEAH-nah) and *bacalhau* (bah-kah-LAW) are prime examples of traditional Brazilian cuisine. *Camarão a bahiana* (spiced shrimp) is a dish brought to Brazil by African slaves and *bacalhoada* (bah-kah-LWAH-dah)—codfish stew with potatoes, tomatoes, and all sorts of seasonings—was brought to Brazil by the Portuguese.

Each state in Brazil is proud of it's own regional cuisine. In Bahia seafood is the specialty. There you can enjoy *vatapá* (vah-tah-PAH), a delicious fish pudding made of bread, ginger, peanuts, cashews, and olive oil. The specialty of Rio Grande do Sul is the famous *churasco* (shoo-RAHS-koh), a variety of meats barbecued over charcoal and served in the many *churrascarias* (shoo-rahs-kah-REE-ahs) all over Brazil. Rio de Janeiro is the place to savor *feijoada* (fey-SHWA-dah), a combination of black beans, beef, pork, and sausage served as a stew. Originally a slave dish, it is always served with rice, orange slices, *farofa* (fah-ROH-fah) and finely shredded kale. Many would consider *feijoada* the national dish of Brazil.

CHILE

Like Argentina, Chile's cuisine is a reflection of its European immigrants' culinary traditions as well as its indigenous foods. *Cazuela* (kah-SWEH-lah), a stew-like soup made with meat (pork, beef, turkey, or chicken with the bone), squash, corn on the cob, potatoes and other vegetables reflects the love of hearty country cooking. Chile has one of the largest fishing industries in South America. With an annual catch of about 6.5 million metric tons, it is not surprising that seafood is an important element of Chilean cuisine. Dishes such as *locos* (LOH-kohs), large-size abalone, *choritos al vapor* (choh-REE-tohs ahl vah-POHR), mussels steamed in white wine, or *chupo de centolla* (CHOO-poh deh sehn-TOH-yah), king crab, are definitely worth sampling. Chileans also eat a lot of pork, and, although their wines have received a lot of attention and recognition abroad, Chileans themselves are not great wine connoisseurs.

MEXICO

Mexican cuisine is as diverse and varied as its culture and history. Its cuisine is more than a set of recipes, it is a manifestation of the geography, characteristics, and ingredients exclusive to Mexico. Europeans were introduced to tomatoes, potatoes, pumpkins, squash, avocados, turkey, chocolate, vanilla, corn, and other foods by way of the Maya Indians. Corn formed the backbone of Maya cuisine in the form of *tamales* (tah-MAH-lehs), *tortillas* (tohr-TEE-yahs), and *atole* (ah-TOH-leh), a corn-based breakfast drink. No other cuisine has *antojitos* (ahn-toh-HEE-tohs), *moles* (MOH-lehs), or *salsas* (SAHL-sahs) made in the traditional *molcajetes* (mohl-kah-HEH-tehs) (mortars) quite like Mexico's. *Antojitos* (literally: "small cravings") come from the mixture of cheese, beef, pork, and chicken meat (introduced by the Spaniards), and the indigenous tortilla, beans, peppers, tomatoes, and aromatic herbs such as *epazote* (eh-pah-SOH-teh) and *cilantro* (see-LAHN-troh). *Tacos* (TAH-kohs), *frijoles refritos* (free-HOH-lehs rreh-FREE-tohs), *quesadillas* (keh-sah-DEE-yahs), *tamales* (tah-MAH-lehs), and *burritos* (boo-RREE-tohs) can be classified as *antojitos*. *Mole* (MOH-leh) comes from the Aztec word *molli* (MOH-yee) meaning concoction, stew, or sauce. It is an exceptionally complex dish made with chiles, nuts, seeds, vegetables, spices, and chocolate. There are hundreds of different types of *mole* ranging from *mole poblano* (MOH-leh poh-BLAH-noh) (from the state of Puebla) to *mole verde* (MOH-leh VEHR-deh) (green mole). Although the thousands of Mexican dishes cannot be described entirely in this guide, the more common ones are.

PERU

Peruvian cuisine varies from region to region, with seafood dominating the coastal region. Food can be spicy and rich in flavor, variety, and complexity. *Ceviche* is one of the most famous and traditional dishes of Peru. *Ceviche* (seh-VEE-cheh) is raw fish marinated with lemons, onions, and *ají* (ah-HEE) (Peruvian salsa). Fish dishes can be prepared *a lo macho* (AH loh MAH-choh), in spicy seafood sauce, and *a la chorillana* (AH lah choh-ree-YAH-nah), fried with onions and tomatoes. The variety of Peruvian seafood dishes is endless, everything from *pulpo* (POOL-poh), octopus, to *calamares fritos* (kah-lah-MAH-rehs FREE-tohs), fried squid, and *angulas* (ahn-GOO-lahs), baby eels. You'll be interested to know that, thanks to its Asian population, Peru has some of the best Chinese and Japanese food in all of Latin America.

SPAIN
—⁓—

Spanish food is as varied and sophisticated as any other European cuisine. Spain is an agricultural country with rich vineyards and olive groves, and its geographical diversity combined with its Roman and Moorish influences contribute to its culinary uniqueness. One of the most popular Spanish culinary traditions are the *tapas* (TAH-pahs). *Tapas* are small portions of food that are traditionally eaten before lunch or dinner. Originally from the Andalucía region, their popularity has grown not only in Spain, but in the United States as well. They can be eaten as appetizers or as meals in themselves. You can find excellent *tapas* restaurants in most major cities in the United States. If you are unsure of what to order, ask your waiter or waitress to recommend three or four of their tastiest and most popular *tapas*, and don't forget to order a pitcher of *sangría* (sahn-GREE-ah) to go along with them.

Gazpacho (gahs-PAH-choh) is a chilled soup made by mixing tomatoes, onions, peppers, cucumbers, garlic, and olive oil. The Spanish *tortilla* (tohr-TEE-yah) is similar to an omelette which is filled with any combination of potatoes, cured ham, tomatoes, and other ingredients. Perhaps the most famous Spanish dish is *paella* (pah-EH-yah), which consists of rice, meat, fish, shellfish, and vegetables flavored with saffron. *Cocidos* (koh-SEE-dohs) are meat stews made with meats, legumes, and vegetables. Spaniards—especially the Andalucians and Galicians—are known for their vast consumption of fish and seafood.

Aperitifs

DRINKING CUSTOMS VARY around the Spanish-speaking countries. The Spanish might have one of their native sherries, *jerez* (he-REHS), or a common European aperitif such as Campari or Vermouth. Latin Americans will more likely have a mixed drink from their own country or another American favorite, such as gin-based drinks or Scotch. Popular throughout South America are various versions of sugarcane liquors, such as *ron* (ROHN), rum, and *aguardiente* (ahgwar-DYEN-te). In Mexico, tequila dominates, especially in the famous Margarita. Wine is always a popular drink in Spain, and Chile and Argentina are producing excellent wines at moderate prices. Whatever your choice, relax and prepare yourself for a pleasant meal.

Cachaça (ka-SHAH-zah)

Cachaça is a Brazilian liquor made from distilled sugarcane juice. While rum is distilled from molasses, *cachaça* is distilled directly from the juice of the unrefined sugarcane. Brazil has 4,000 brands of *cachaça*. It is one of the most widely consumed drinks in Brazil, second only to beer.

Chinchón and *Ojén* (cheen-CHOHN, oh-HEHN)

These are anise-flavored liquors of Spain, similar to the pastis of France, and are usually drunk with water.

Jerez (heh-REHS)

The famous Spanish wine originated in southwest Andalucía, in the region of Jerez. This sherry wine is fortified with brandy made from the same grapes. The very driest is *fino,* and the next driest is *amontillado,* also known as dry or cocktail sherry. Either is excellent as an aperitif. The heavier-bodied and sweeter *olorosos* and cream sherries are dessert wines.

Mezcal (mehs-KAHL)

Tequila made outside the geographical limitations established by the Mexican government for true tequila production.

Pisco (PEES-koh)

Pisco is a type of brandy popular in Peru and Chile. A pisco sour is a drink made from *pisco,* lemon juice, ice, and salt.

PHRASES FOR ORDERING DRINKS IN SPANISH:

en las rocas EHN lahs ROH-kahs	*on the rocks*
con soda KOHN SOH-dah	*with soda*
con agua KOHN AH-gwah	*with water*
vino tinto VEE-noh TEEN-toh	*red wine*
vino blanco VEE-noh BLAHN-koh	*white wine*

Pulque (POOL-keh)

A milky-white Mexican alcoholic beverage fermented from the juice of the agave plant. It predates the arrival of the Spaniards and the knowledge of distilling. Rarely seen in the United States because of its low alcohol content and susceptibility to spoilage.

Ron (RHON)

Ron (rum) is an alcoholic beverage produced by the distillation of various fermented cane sugar products. The most common mixtures used in making rum consist of molasses and water or sugar and water. Another type of rum is made by fermenting a mixture of the scum formed when the raw juice of the sugarcane is heated with molasses, water, and "dunder," the residue left after the refining of sugar. When distilled, rum is a white or straw-colored spirit varying in strength from 80 to 150 proof (40 to 75 percent alcohol). *Cuba libres* (KOO-bah LEE-brehs), rum and Coke drinks, are very popular throughout Latin America. Most rum for export is made in Barbados, Trinidad, Jamaica, Guyana, Cuba, and Puerto Rico.

Sangría (sahn-GREE-ah)

A red wine punch flavored with fresh citrus fruit and served in ice-filled pitchers. A refreshing drink suited for the scorching heat of southern Spain.

Tequila (teh-KEE-lah)

A Mexican spirit distilled from the fermented liquid of the crushed bases of the small agave plant, the *agave tequilana* (also called the American aloe or century plant). The white or clear tequila is generally used for mixed drinks. The pale gold tequila, aged for about a year, is mixed or drunk straight, and the aged tequilas, the *añejos* (ah-NYEH-hos), aged six to eight years, are drunk straight. The Mexican way of drinking tequila is to hold a lime in the left hand and place a little salt in the well at the base of the thumb and index finger of the same hand. Hold the tequila glass in the other hand. Lick the salt, swallow some tequila, then suck the lime.

Margaritas are cocktails traditionally made with tequila, triple sec (an orange liqueur), and lime juice. A cocktail glass is rimmed with salt and the ingredients are shaken and strained into the glass. It's a tasty and refreshing drink. The American penchant is for making frozen margaritas, which disguise the flavor of tequila and dilute the alcohol.

¡Salud!	*Cheers!*
¡sah-LOOD!	
¡A tu salud!	*To your health!*
¡ah too sah-LOOD!	
¡Arriba, abajo, al centro, pa' dentro!	*Bottoms up!*
¡ah-REE-bah ah-BAH-ho ahl SEHN-troh PAH DEHN-troh!	

Appetizers

IN SPAIN AND THROUGHOUT Latin America, meals are a big deal. A one-course meal would be unthinkable. As in so many other cultures, they spend a lot of time eating. (Don't you wish we did?) Why don't you consider enjoying a long, leisurely dinner at a Latin restaurant? It is not unusual for a meal to last two to three hours in Spain and Latin American countries. Just remember, Spaniards and Latin Americans don't eat as early as we do. It's customary to have dinner quite late, 8:00 P.M. or later, even as late as midnight (this is especially true in Spain). In those countries, you will find the restaurants practically empty before 9:00 P.M., and jamming at midnight. So get yourself in the mood, start late, and eat slowly. Drink just enough wine, but not too much. Linger as long as you like and take in the ambience. When you wake up the next day, maybe you'll understand just a little more about Latin romance and intrigue.

Antojitos (ahn-toh-HEE-tohs) are Mexico's version of the *tapas*/appetizers. Many of the dishes usually considered Mexican entrées are actually *antojitos*. As mentioned previously, *tamales, quesadillas, tacos, burritos, totopos* (chips) *y guacamole, tostadas, sopes,* and other dishes made with Mexico's staple foods (tortillas, tomatoes, chiles, onions, cheese, and beans) can usually be served as *antojitos*.

Aguacate a la valenciana (ah-guah-KAH-teh AH LAH ba-lehn-SYAH-nah)

Avocado with grapefruit and vinaigrette.

Almejas a la marinera (ahl-MEH-hahs ah lah mah-ree-NEH-rah)

Clams steamed with white wine, garlic, and herbs.

Aros de cebolla ocultos (ah-ROHS deh seh-BOH-yah oh-KOOL-tohs)

Fried onion rings, in batter.

IN THE BEGINNING:

Una mesa para dos personas.	A table for two.
OO-nah MEH-sah PAH-rah DOHS pehr-SOH-nahs.	
¿Puede traer . . .	Can you bring . . .
PWEH-deh trah-HER . . .	
la carta?	the menu?
lah KAHR-tah?	
la lista de vinos?	the wine list?
lah LEES-tah deh VEE-nohs?	
Quisiera . . .	I'd like . . .
kee-SYEH-rah . . .	

Bolitas de queso (boh-LEE-tahs deh KEH-soh)
Fried battered cheese balls.

Caracoles a la andaluza (kah-rah-KOH-lehs ah lah
ahn-dah-LOO-zah)
Stewed snails with almonds and paprika. This is a
surprisingly wonderful way to enjoy snails.

Ceviche chileno (seh-VEE-cheh chee-LEH-noh)
Marinated raw fish, Chilean style (with tomatoes,
onions, lemon and orange juices, hot pepper).

Coctel de gambas/camarones (KOHK-tel deh GAHM-
bahs/kah-mah-ROH-nehs)
Shrimp cocktail.

Cogollos de Tudela (koh-GOH-yohs deh too-DEH-lah)
Hearts of romaine.

Empanadas (ehm-pah-NAH-dahs)
As described in the *tapas* section (page 141),
empanadas come in various
sizes and can be filled with
almost anything. While
many are used as *tapas,* they
make great appetizers or even
main courses.

Empanada berciana (ehm-pah-NAH-dah behr-SYAH-
nah)
Pork and chorizo pie.

Empanada asturiana (ehm-pah-NAH-dah ahs-too-
RYAH-na)
Chorizo pie, an Asturian specialty.

Empanada de berberechos (ehm-pah-NAH-dah deh
behr-beh-REH-chos)
Clam or cockle pie.

Empanada de espinacas (ehm-pah-NAH-dah deh ehs-pee-NAH-kahs)
Spinach pie.

Empanada de lomo (ehm-pah-NAH-dah deh LOH-moh)
Pork loin pie.

Empanada mallorquina (ehm-pah-NAH-dah mah-yohr-KEE-nah)
Lamb pie.

Endibias al roquefort (ehn-DEE-byahs ahl ROHK-fohrt)
Belgian endive with Roquefort cheese.

Entremeses variados (ehn-tre-MEH-sehs bah-RYA-dohs)
Assorted appetizers.

Escabeche de bonito (ehs-kah-BEH-che deh boh-NEE-tohs)
Pickled bonito tuna.

Fritos de Berenjena (FREE-tohs deh beh-rehn-HEH-nah)
Fried eggplant pieces.

Hojaldrados de chorizo (oh-hal-DRAH-dohs deh choh-REE-soh)
Chorizo in puff pastry.

Jamón con tomate (hah-MOHN KOHN toh-MAH-teh)
Ham with tomatoes and peppers.

Nidos de patata (NEE-dohs deh pah-TAH-tah)
Fried potato nests.

Pastel (pahs-TEHL)
A pastel may be a cake, a pie, a pâté, or a terrine.

Pastel de carne (pahs-TEHL deh KAHR-neh)
Meat pie.

Pastel de liebre (pahs-TEHL deh LYEH-bre)
Rabbit pie.

Pastel de Perdiz (pahs-TEHL deh pehr-DEES)
Pâté of partridge, made with partridge, veal, pork, pork fat, truffles, and spices.

Pastel de puerros y gambas (pahs-TEHL deh PWEH-rrohs e GAHM-bahs)
A mold of shrimp and leeks in a custard. Very delicate and light.

Repollo relleno de salchicha (reh-POH-yoh rreh-YEH-noh deh sahl-CHEE-chah)
Cabbage stuffed with sausage.

Riñones a la Cantabra (ree-NYOH-nehs AH LAH kahn-TAH-brah)
Lamb kidneys on a skewer with bacon, sausage, and mushrooms.

Sobrasada (soh-brah-SAH-dah)
Chorizo spread, made by puréeing chorizo and extra pork fat. You shouldn't have asked.

Terrina de conejo (teh-REE-nah deh coh-NEH-hoh)
Rabbit terrine.

Torta de chicharrones (TOHR-tah deh chee-chah-RROH-nehs)
Pork-rind torte.

Tortitas de arroz (tohr-TEE-tahs deh ah-RROHS)
Rice pancakes made from rice and cream sauce, sautéed in olive oil.

Trucha en aceite (TROO-chah EHN ah-SAY-teh)
Fried trout fillets in olive oil, served cold.

Tapas

IN RECENT YEARS, the Spanish snacks known as *tapas* (TAH-pahs) have become especially popular throughout the United States. In Spain they're eaten as a snack or light meal while standing at the bar and range from something as simple as olives to something as sophisticated as poached octopus vinaigrette. In the United States, Spanish restaurants often offer *tapas* in the dining room as an addition or alternative to traditional appetizers and entrées. Non-Spanish restaurants are starting to use the *tapas* concept of the small portion so diners can "graze" with abandon. The selections below represent some of the more popular Spanish *tapas* among the thousands possible. Order away!

Aceitunas alinadas (ah-say-TOO-nahs ah-lee-NAH-dahs)
> Marinated olives.

Aceitunas rellenas (ah-say-TOO-nahs rreh-YEH-nahs)
> Stuffed (green) olives.

Albóndigas (ahl-BOHN-dee-gahs)

Meatballs made from pork, garlic, onion, parsley, bread crumbs, and eggs. Very good dipped in spicy mayonnaise.

Almendras saladas (ahl-MEHN-drahs sah-lah-dahs)

Fried salted almonds. What better food to go with a cold beer?

Angulas a la bilbaina (ahn-goo-lahs AH LAH beel-BYE-nah)

Baby eels sauteed in oil with hot pepper. Very popular in Spain. Some Americans have trouble with the idea of eating eel, but they're really worth a try.

Atún en escabeche (ah-TOON EHN ehs-kah-BEH-cheh)

Pickled tuna. Absolutely delicious!

Barquitas (bahr-KEE-tahs)

Boat-shaped pastries, often stuffed or filled with any number of possible ingredients, such as vegetables, mousse, seafood, or meat.

Boquerones en vinagre (boh-keh-ROH-nehs EHN bee-NAH-greh)

Pickled smelts or sardines in vinegar.

Buñuelos (boo-NYWEH-lohs)

Fritters, made by frying small scoops of heavy batter with various ingredients mixed in. They seem to be the ideal bar food!

? DID YOU KNOW?

You'll notice that meat is a major ingredient in Spanish and Latin American cooking. This is not surprising, since Spain and Latin America are great producers of beef and pork. Also, they use a great deal more organ meats than Americans do. Some of these dishes are just outstanding, so open your mind and your mouth, and enjoy!

Buñuelos de chorizo (boo-NYWE-LOHS deh choh-REE-soh)

Spicy sausage fritters, in which chorizo is chopped up and mixed in the batter.

Buñuelos de bacalao (boo-NYWE-lohs deh bah-kah-LAH-oh)

Fritters made with dried and salted cod. These are a good way to eat salt cod, which can be a bit strong to the uninitiated.

Buñuelos de queso (boo-NYWE-lohs deh KEH-soh)

Cheese fritters.

Calamares en su tinta (kah-lah-MAH-rehs EHN SOO TEEN-tah)

Squid cooked in its own ink.

Calamares fritos (kah-lah-MAH-rehs FREE-tohs)

Fried squid.

Canapé de anchoa y pimiento (kah-nah-PEH deh ahn-CHO-ah E pee-MYEHN-toh)

Anchovy and pimiento canapé.

Caracoles de Borgona (kah-rah-KOH-lehs deh bohr-GOH-nah)

Snails with butter, garlic, and parsley. Snails are extremely popular in Spain, and this is a most delicious way to eat them.

Caracoles en salsa picante (kah-rah-KOH-lehs EHN SAHL-sah pee-KAHN-teh)

Snails in hot sauce.

Cebollitas al limón (seh-boh-YEE-tahs AHL lee-MOHN)

Small white onions in lemon and oil.

Champinones al ajillo (chahm-pee-NYOH-nehs AHL ah-HEE-yoh)
Mushrooms with garlic.

Chorizo a la sidra (choh-REE-soh AH LAH SEE-drah)
Chorizos with apples in hard cider.

Delicias de queso (deh-LEE-see-ahs deh KEH-soh)
Fried cheese balls.

Empanada de carne (ehm-pah-NAH-dah deh KAHR-neh)
Ground beef, garlic, pepper, tomato, and spices in pastry.

Empanadilla (ehm-pah-nah-DEE-yah)
Small turnover or pie. Diminutive of *empanada,* the famous larger turnover or pie. Depending on where you encounter these, *empanadas* may be just about any size. They are one of the hot foods in the United States today, a delicious and versatile way to serve anything that can be put in a crust. Only the imagination limits what goes into these divine little pastries.

Empanadillas de atún (ehm-pah-nah-DEE-yahs deh ah-TOON)
Tuna turnovers.

Empanadillas de ternera (ehm-pah-nah-DEE-yahs deh tehr-NEH-rah)
Spicy ground veal and tomato turnovers.

Gambas a la plancha (GAHM-bahs AH LAH PLAHN-chah)
Broiled shrimp.

Gambas al ajillo (GAHM-bahs AHL ah-HEE-yoh)
Shrimp with garlic.

Gambas rebosadas (GAHM-bahs rreh-boh-SAH-dahs)
Breaded and fried shrimp.

Huevas de pescado (WEH-vahs deh pehs-KAH-doh)
   Fish roe (cured).

Mejillones en salsa verde (meh-hee-YOH-nehs EHN
SAHL-sah VEHR-deh)
   Mussels in green sauce.

Mejillones rellenos (meh-hee-YOH-nehs rre-YEH-
nohs)
   Stuffed mussels, generally finished with a white
   sauce.

Pelotas en salsa roja (peh-LOH-tahs EHN SAHL-sah
RROH-hah)
   Meatballs in red sherry sauce.

Pepinillos en vinagre (peh-pee-NEE-yohs EHN bee-
NAH-greh)
   Gherkins in vinegar.

Pepito de ternera (peh-PEE-toh deh tehr-NEH-rah)
   Grilled veal sandwich.

Riñones al jerez (rree-NYOH-nehs AHL heh-REHS)
   Veal kidneys in sherry sauce.

Sepia con cebolla (SEH-peeah COHN seh-BOH-yah)
   Cuttlefish with onions. Cuttlefish is similar to
   octopus.

Soups

THE BEST SPANISH and Latin American soups seem to be the hearty, rustic soups typical of the countryside. There are fish, bean, and meat soups that really zing with flavor. Some lighter varieties, such as consommés, garlic soups, and lighter fish soups, are also delicious. The world-popular *gazpacho* is an excellent summer dish and is such a part of Spanish culinary tradition that you can even buy it in a carton in many McDonald's restaurants throughout Spain. You will find that throughout Latin America, lots of different soups reflect ingredients that are plentiful and indigenous to each country.

Different words imply different types of soups. *Sopa* means simply soup. *Caldo* can be a clear broth, a soup made with a clear broth, a consommé, or even a light stew. A *chupe* is a South American spicy soup, and a *potaje* is a thick, hearty soup or stew.

Ajiaco (ah-HEEEAH-koh)
Potato, pea, and avocado soup.

Ajiaco santafereño (ah-HEEEAH-koh sahn-tah-feh-REH-nyoh)
Chicken, potato, and corn soup from the Bogotá region of Colombia. Three types of Colombian

potatoes are required for this specialty: pastusos, sabaneros, and criollos.

Albondigas al caldillo (ahl-bohn-DEE-gahs AHL kahl-DEE-yoh)
Mexican meatballs in broth.

Caldo de pescado (KAHL-doh deh pehs-KAH-doh)
Fish broth.

Caldo gallego (KAHL-doh gah-YEH-goh)
A specialty of Galicia made of white beans, potatoes, greens, and beef.

Chupe de mariscos (CHOO-peh deh mah-REES-kohs)
Chilean shrimp and scallop soup.

Fabada asturiana (fah-BAH-dah ahs-too-RYAH-nah)
Lima or butter bean stew with various sausages and cuts of pork.

Gazpacho (gahs-PAH-choh)
A cold puréed tomato soup with onions, peppers, garlic, olive oil, and cucumbers. *Gazpacho* is a very refreshing, summer "liquid salad." We tend to add hot pepper, something which is not part of the original Andalusian recipe.

Mondongo (mohn-DOHN-goh)
Pepper pot: spicy tripe and vegetable soup.

Potaje de guisantes (poh-TAH-heh deh ghee-SAHN-tehs)
Pea soup.

Sopa criolla de pollo (SOH-pah KRYOH-yah deh POH-yoh)
Argentine chicken and vegetable soup.

Sopa de aguacate (SOH-pah deh ah-gwah-KAH-teh)
Avocado soup.

Sopa de ajo (SOH-pah deh AH-ho)
Spicy garlic soup.

Sopa de albondiguillas (SOH-pah deh ahl-bohn-dee-GHEE-yahs)

Meatball soup.

Sopa de cebollas y almendras (SOH-pah deh she-BOH-yahs E ahl-MEHN-drahs)

Onion and almond soup.

Sopa de elote (SOH-pah deh eh-LOH-teh)

Corn soup.

Sopa de flor de calabaza (SOH-pah deh FLOHR deh kah-la-BAH-sah)

Squash blossom soup.

Sopa de legumbres (SOH-pah deh leh-GOOM-brehs)

Thick vegetable soup.

Sopa de lentejas (SOH-pah deh lehn-TEH-has)

Lentil soup.

Sopa de manioc (SOH-pah deh mah-NYOHK)

A rich beef broth with some tapioca added, along with flaked coconut and cream. See the glossary for a discussion of tapioca.

Sopa de pan en cazuela (SOH-pah deh PAHN EHN kah-SWEH-lah)

Bread soup in casserole, made with beef broth and milk. In each casserole are placed sliced cheese, sautéed onions and garlic, and crumbled toast. The broth is poured in, and slices of bread and a raw egg are placed on each dish, which is then baked. Delicious!

Sopa de pescado y almendras (SOH-pah deh pehs-KAH-doh E ahl-MEHN-drahs)

Fish and almond soup.

Sopa de tortilla (SOH-**pah deh tohr**-TEE-**yah**)
Soup made with tomatoes, onions, and cheese, with fried tortillas added.

Sopa de yautia (SOH-**pah deh** YOW-**teeah**)
Sweet potato soup.

I NEED . . .

¿Puede traer . . .	*Could you bring . . .*
PWEH-deh trah-HER . . .	
una servilleta?	*a napkin?*
OO-nah sehr-bee-YEH-tah?	
un tenedor?	*a fork?*
oon teh-neh-DOHR?	
una cuchara?	*a spoon?*
OO-nah koo-CHAH-rah?	
un cuchillo?	*a knife?*
oon koo-CHEE-yoh?	

Cheese

SPANISH CHEESES MIRROR to a great extent other European cheeses. Although there is a great variety of Spanish cheeses, many can only be found in the regions where they are made. The hard cheeses of the La Mancha region, as well as the *manchego* and *cabrales* cheeses, are particularly tasty and should be sampled when available. As in Spain, there is a great variety of regional cheeses in Latin America, with Mexico offering the greatest variety. Many of the cheeses are fresh, resembling mozzarella, farmer's cheeses, cream cheese, or crumbly-type cheeses like feta.

Añejo enchilado (ah-NYEH-hoh ehn-chee-LAH-doh)
Commonly used for stuffing enchiladas, burritos, and tacos. It has a mild and slightly spicy flavor and can be easily shredded or grated.

Cabrales (kah-BRAH-lehs)
Aged cheese, from semi-cured to cured, made from whole unpasteurized cow's, goat's, and sheep's milk, depending on the season.

Cotija (koh-TEE-hah)
This cheese is known as the "Parmesan of Mexico." It was originally made from goat's milk but today cow's milk is preferred. Strongly flavored, firm and perfect for grating, cotija is commonly used as a garnish to liven up *antojitos*.

Manchego (mahn-CHEH-goh)

Aged cheese, semi-cured to cured, made exclusively with raw or pasteurized sheep's milk.

Oaxaca (wah-HAH-kah)

Also known as *asadero, oaxaca* cheese is semi-soft, white, and stringy. It melts well and is excellent for quesadillas, sandwiches, and pizza.

Panela (pah-NEH-lah)

The most popular fresh cheese in Mexico. *Panela* cheese is mild, white, and crumbly. It is commonly crushed and used over *antojitos*.

Queso de Burgos (KEH-soh deh BOOR-gohs)

A mild cheese from sheep's milk.

Queso fresco (KEH-soh FREHS-koh)

This cheese is based on the burgos cheese from Spain. Very mild with a fresh acidity. Queso fresco (fresh cheese) is also great on *antojitos*.

Requesón (rreh-keh-SOHN)

Unsalted sheep or goat's milk cheese.

Roncal (rrohn-KAHL)

Also *queso del Valle del Roncal*. Aged for at least four months, and cured, made from sheep's milk. The traditional artisanal production is passed down from one generation to the next.

Eggs

EGGS ARE PERHAPS the single most important food in Spain. They're included in practically every meal. Latin Americans, too, have followed in this custom and consume large amounts of eggs, many in the same dishes. Spanish and Latin American restaurants in the United States don't generally offer so much in the way of eggs because they don't fit into elegant settings, and Americans tend to eat eggs mostly at breakfast. Also, many of these egg dishes are lunch or *tapas* offerings, so you won't encounter them on dinner menus. Here are a few common dishes of this most versatile food.

Huasvulchi (wahs-VOOL-chee)
   Mexican eggs, tomatoes, and cheese, a Holy Week specialty.

Huevos a la flamenca (WEH-vohs AH LAH flah-MEHN-kah)
   Baked eggs with vegetables and chorizo.

Huevos a la mexicana (WEH-vohs AH LAH meh-hee-KAH-nah)
   Scrambled eggs with onion and tomato sauce.

Huevos duros (WEH-vohs DOO-rohs)
   Hard-boiled eggs.

Huevos en salsa agria (WEH-vohs EHN SAHL-sah AH-gryah)
   Hard-boiled eggs in a sweet and sour sauce.

Huevos fritos (WEH-vohs FREE-tohs)
Fried eggs (whole eggs deep-fried in oil).

Huevos pasados por agua (WEH-vohs pah-SAH-dohs POHR AH-gwah)
Poached eggs.

Huevos rancheros (WEH-vohs rrahn-CHEH-rohs)
Fried eggs on tortilla topped with hot tomato sauce.

Huevos rellenos (WEH-vohs rreh-YEH-nohs)
Stuffed eggs. They may be stuffed with shrimp, fish, meat, or vegetables.

Huevos revueltos (WEH-vohs reh-BWEHL-tohs)
Scrambled eggs.

Llapingachos (yah-peen-GAH-chohs)
Ecuadorian potato pancakes with poached eggs.

Piparrada (pee-pah-RRAH-dah)
Eggs scrambled with tomato and peppers.

Tortilla asturiana (tohr-TEE-yah ahs-too-RYAH-nah)
Tuna, onion, and tomato omelette.

Tortilla a la barcelonesa (tohr-TEE-yah AH LAH bahr-she-loh-NEH-sah)
Omelette with chicken livers, ham, tomatoes, cheese sauce, spinach, and potatoes.

Tortilla Ampurdanesa (tohr-TEE-yah ahm-poor-dah-NEH-sah)
Omelette with white beans.

Tortilla andaluza (tohr-TEE-yah ahn-dah-loo-sah)
Omelette with tomatoes, ham, peppers, and mushrooms.

Tortilla buena mujer (tohr-TEE-yah BWEH-nah moo-HEHR)
Omelette with bacon, onions, and mushrooms.

Tortilla chistorra (tohr-TEE-yah chees-TOH-rah)
Omelette with chorizo sausage.

Tortilla de angulas (tohr-TEE-yah deh ahn-GOO-lahs)
Omelette of tiny eels.

Tortilla española (tohr-TEE-yah ehs-pah-NYOH-lah)
This is pretty much the national dish of Spain, and it seems to be becoming better known in the United States. Sliced potatoes and onions are cooked in a flat omelette. But it's not as simple as it sounds: the potatoes and onions are first fried in olive oil, and the process of making the tortilla involves lots of flipping. The finished product, usually served at room temperature, has a delightful fragrance of the ingredients and a smooth, slightly juicy texture. They make great tapas when cut into small wedges and can serve as lunch or dinner in larger portions. Try one as soon as you can. Have a nice glass of a light-bodied red wine or a bone-dry white of light to medium body. Or even a beer. Enjoy!

Tortillas are different in Spain and Mexico. In Mexico, a tortilla is a pancake-like disk made from either flour or corn and pressed very thin. The Mexican tortilla can be filled with various ingredients; a corn tortilla makes an enchilada and a flour tortilla makes a burrito. Tortillas are an ever-present element of a Mexican meal, similar to a French baguette. In Spain, a tortilla is basically a frittata, or an open-faced omelette.

Breads

BREADS ARE EXTREMELY IMPORTANT in the entire Spanish-speaking world. In every country and every region, local ingredients play a prominent part in what kind of bread is made. For example, in northern Spain corn and rye are used extensively, while in central Spain, in Castilla, fine wheat is grown and used in bread making. In South America, corn and wheat are both common. It is unusual to make bread at home, as it is in many parts of the world. Bakeries have the proper equipment, and prices are low enough to make it unnecessary to bake bread at home. Indeed, in many of the countries price and quality are regulated by the government.

Arepa (ah-REH-pah)
  Bread made with white or yellow cornmeal and grilled, not baked. Very common in Venezuela and Colombia.

Bolillo (boh-LEE-yoh)
  Mexican crusty bread, made into a small loaf.

Pan candeal (PAHN kahn-DEHAHL)
  Country-style bread, dense and crusty.

Pan de cebada (PAHN deh seh-BAH-dah)
  Corn and barley bread, very dense.

Pan de pueblo (PAHN deh PWEH-bloh)
  Basic crusty bread in Spain, made into a long loaf.

Just what are they? *Burritos, enchiladas, tacos. Burritos* are flour tortillas filled and rolled up. Typical fillings are refried beans, shredded meats, lettuce, tomatoes, and cheese. *Tacos* are corn tortillas filled and folded. As for *burritos,* typical fillings are beans and shredded meats. Most Americans are used to the *tacos dorados,* fried tacos, in which the corn tortilla is fried until crisp, then filled. *Enchiladas* are corn tortillas dipped in a spicy tomato sauce, fried, and filled with cheese or shredded meats.

Pan de yuca (PAHN deh YOO-kah)

Bread made from yuca starch and fresh white cheese, moist and tender.

Pan gallego de centeno (PAHN deh sehn-TEH-noh)

Galician rye bread, with wheat flour, rye flour, cornmeal, lard, and caraway seeds.

Quesadilla (keh-sah-DEE-yah)

A tortilla "turnover" filled with cheese and then baked, grilled, or fried. Fillings also include shredded meats or beans.

Tamales (tah-MAH-lehs)

Tamales are a special dish in Mexico, made for special occasions. They are, in their simplest form, just *masa,* a type of cornmeal, mixed with chicken stock and lard, wrapped in corn husks, and steamed. But all sorts of ingredients are added: fish, pumpkin, pineapple, peanuts, rice, chiles, julienne vegetables, etc. Tamales are a wonderful treat dating back to pre-Columbian times.

Tortilla (tohr-TEE-yah)

Mexican flat bread with no leavening, made from either flour or corn. The corn tortilla is most commonly served with dinner.

Vegetables, Salads, Sauces, and Other Preparations

Alio-li (ah-LYOH-lee)
Garlic mayonnaise.

Arroz a la mexicana (ah-RROHS AH LAH meh-hee-KAH-nah)
Browned rice with tomatoes and onions, cooked in chicken broth.

Arroz con azafrán (ah-RROHS KOHN ah-sah-FRAHN)
Saffron rice.

Arroz verde (ah-RROHS BEHR-deh)
Rice with green chile and green tomato.

Budín de elote (boo-DEEN deh eh-LOH-teh)
Corn pudding.

Chilaquiles (chee-lah-KEE-lehs)
Fried tortilla strips mixed with tomato sauce, chiles, onions, and cheese and topped with cheese and cream. Traditional Mexican breakfast or *almuerzo* (11:00 A.M. meal).

 Breakfast, el desayuno, *in Spain and Latin America is very light and comparable to the continental breakfast we are accustomed to.* El almuerzo, *which is usually taken around 11:00 A.M., is a mid-morning snack or lunch.* La comida *is the big meal in Spain and Latin America and is usually taken after 2:00 P.M. As stated previously, Spaniards and Latin Americans eat dinner,* la cena, *much later, usually after 8:00 P.M. and as late as midnight.*

Chiles rellenos (CHEE-lehs rreh-YEH-nohs)
Cheese-stuffed chiles, dipped in egg whites and fried.

Empanada (ehm-pah-NAH-dahs)

Pie or turnover. In Spain, these are popular, and in Latin America they are absolutely indispensable. Throughout Latin America they're the half-moon–shaped turnovers, filled with anything you can think of. You'll see them on non-Latin menus these days because the concept is so simple, and so easy to make delicious. By all means have some if you like pie pastry. Yum yum.

Ensalada a la almoraina (ehn-sah-LAH-dah AH LAH ahl-moh-RYE-nah)

Escarole salad with tomato and cumin dressing.

Ensalada de corazón de palma vinagrette (ehn-sah-LAH-dah deh koh-rah-SOHN deh PAHL-mah)

Hearts of palm in an oil, vinegar, and onion dressing.

(en) escabeche (EHN ehs-kah-BEH-cheh)

Pickled or marinated.

Espinacas con piñones y almendras (ehs-pee-NAH-kahs KOHN pee-NYOH-nehs E ahl-MEHN-drahs)

Spinach with pine nuts and almonds.

Flores de calabaza rellenas (FLOH-rehs deh kah-lah-BAH-sah rreh-YEH-nahs)

Stuffed squash blossoms.

Frijoles charros (free-HOH-lehs CHAH-rrohs)

Beans cooked with beer, chorizo, and pork rinds.

? DID YOU KNOW?

You can find many words in the English language that come from *Náhuatl,* the Aztec language. Words like *xocolatl* (chocolate), *mexica* (Mexican), *chilli* (chili/chile peppers), and *coyotl* (coyote). Can you guess what the word *tomatl* means? If you can, you are one smart *tomato!*

Frijoles mexicanos (free-HOH-lehs meh-hee-KAH-nohs)

Boiled beans seasoned with salt, garlic, and—usually—lard.

Frijoles refritos (free-HOH-lehs rreh-FREE-tohs)

Refried beans, made from mashing cooked pinto beans and cooking in oil or lard. A Mexican staple, they can accompany just about any dish, and are frequently put inside tortillas.

Frituras de yautia (free-TOO-rahs deh YAW-tyah)

Sweet potato fritters.

Guacamole (gwah-kah-MOH-leh)

Mashed avocado, seasoned with condiments. Guacamole has become very popular in the United States in the last few years. It's normally served with tortilla chips.

Habas a la andaluza (AH-bahs AH LAH ahn-dah-LOO-sah)

Lima beans with artichokes, onion, garlic, tomato, saffron, and cumin.

Habas a la catalana (AH-bahs AH LAH kah-tah-LAH-nah)

Fava beans with sausages and mint.

Judias verdes con salsa de tomate (hoo-DEE-ahs BEHR-dehs KOHN SAHL-sah deh toh-MAH-teh)

Green beans in tomato sauce.

Migas (MEE-gahs)

Fried bread croutons.

Nopalitos rellenos (noh-pah-LEE-tohs rreh-YEH-nohs)

Stuffed prickly-pear leaves.

Pastel (pahs-TEHL)

The *empanadas,* pies, originate in Galicia; other areas call them *pasteles.* Also, *pasteles* can mean cake or pâté, or any sort of dish in a casserole or mold.

Patatas en salsa verde (pah-TAH-tahs EHN SAHL-sah BEHR-deh)
Potatoes sautéed with onion and garlic, and finished with water and parsley.

Patatas rellenas con queso (pah-TAH-tahs rreh-YEH-nahs KOHN KEH-soh)
Potato-cheese croquettes, made into balls and fried.

Pepinillos en vinagre (peh-pee-NEE-yohs EHN bee-NAH-greh)
Pickled cucumbers.

Pisto manchego (PEES-toh mahn-CHEH-goh)
Zucchini, green pepper, and tomato medley, a dish from La Mancha.

Salpicón de langostino y tomate (sahl-pee-KOHN deh lahn-gohs-TEE-noh E toh-MAH-teh)
Shrimp and tomato in sherry vinaigrette. The sherry vinegar adds a wonderful nutty taste that complements the shrimp.

Sopes (SOH-pehs)
Masa dough disks grilled or fried and topped with shredded meats, salsa, cheese, and sometimes cream and shredded lettuce.

Taquitos (tah-KEE-tohs)
Rolled tacos stuffed with shredded meats and fried.

Cold Meats and Sausages

SAUSAGE IS USED in lots of Spanish and Latin American dishes. It comes in both fresh and cured styles. The cold meats and sausages from Spain are world-renowned and can be served as *tapas* or appetizers.

Butifarra (boo-tee-FAH-rrah)
Butifarra is a spicy Catalan sausage usually seasoned with cinnamon and cloves.

Chorizo (choh-REE-soh)
In Spain *chorizo* is a spicy paprika sausage. Mexican *chorizo* is very spicy and once cooked looks more like ground beef than a sausage. In Mexico it is usually served with eggs for breakfast.

Jamón serrano (hah-MOHN seh-RRAH-noh)
A cured ham served as an appetizer or *tapa*, usually accompanied by cheese and olives.

Morcilla (mohr-SEE-yah)
Morcilla is a sausage made with pig's blood, rice, and lard. It's much tastier than it sounds!

Vegetarians may have some challenge in Spanish and Latin American restaurants, but with some creativity and flexibility there should be no major problem. There are many egg-based dishes, and breads abound. Rice is invariably available, and various vegetables, both raw and cooked, can fill out the meal. Keep in mind that many Spanish and Latin American dishes are fried with animal fat, and many of the soups and sauces use a beef or chicken broth base. Vegans may have a tough time of it unless they call ahead—always a good idea for *any* special requests.

Entrées

ASSUMING YOU STILL have room for dinner, here comes the entrée! Both meat and seafood are eaten extensively throughout Spain and Latin America. Every region makes use of the products available locally. When the chefs come to the United States, they adapt similar products available here into their traditional dishes. The results aren't quite the same as in their home countries, but that's no deterrent to delicious food.

> **DID YOU KNOW?**
> Only some of the Spanish and Mexican dishes are spicy. Highly spiced food is more a product of Tex-Mex and the American Southwest than of Mexico. While the Mexicans are no strangers to hot peppers, they tend to use them more prudently than American westerners. Most Spanish food is not unduly piquant.

MEAT AND POULTRY ENTRÉES

Anticuchos (ahn-tee-KOO-chohs)
Skewered barbecued meat.

Arroz con pollo (ah-RROHS KOHN POH-yoh)
Saffron rice with chicken. This dish originated in Spain but is served throughout Latin America. In addition to the chicken, onions, bell peppers, garlic, and peas are mixed in with the rice. In Spain they insist on using their short-grain rice, but in Latin America they use whatever rice they normally use, depending on the country. This one-dish meal is luscious and filling. *Arroz con pollo* is a

specialty of Caribbean countries like Cuba, Puerto Rico, Venezuela, and the Dominican Republic.

Callos a la andaluza (KAH-yohs AH LAH ahn-dah-LOO-sah)

Tripe in a sauce of mint, garbanzo beans, parsley, onions, tomato, pimiento, ham, and sausage.

You will find a great deal more organ meats in Spanish and Latin American cuisine than in the United States. Although some people may have a strong aversion to some of these dishes, those who are a bit more daring will be duly rewarded.

Callos a la madrileña (KAH-yohs AH LAH mah-dree-LEH-nyah)

Tripe stew with calves' feet, ham, and sausages.

Cariucho (kah-RYOU-choh)

Steak with peanut sauce.

Carne asada (KAHR-neh ah-SAH-dah)

Every country has its version of *carne asada,* but it's usually marinated flank steak cooked on the grill.

Carne claveteada (KAHR-neh klah-veh-TEHAH-dah)

Stuffed steak.

Carne de puerco en adobo (KAHR-neh deh PWER-koh EHN ah-DOH-boh)

Pork loin in achiote and chile sauce.

Carne deshebrada (KAHR-neh deh-seh-BRAH-dah)

Shredded beef.

Carne molida venezolana (KAHR-neh moh-LEE-dah beh-neh-soh-LAH-nah)

Venezuelan meat loaf.

Chiles rellenos con puerco (CHEE-lehs rreh-YEH-nohs KOHN PWER-koh)
Pork-stuffed peppers.

Churrasco rebosado (choo-RRAHS-koh rreh-boh-SAH-doh)
Batter-fried fillet of beef.

Cochinita pibil (koh-chee-NEE-tah pee-BEEL)
Yucatecan barbecued pig, stuffed with fruit, chile, and spices, baked in a pit. *Pib* is the Mayan word for the traditional oven of Yucatán, a pit lined with stones.

Cocido madrileño (koh-SEE-doh mah-dree-LEH-nyoh)
Boiled chicken, meats, and vegetables.

Cordero asado (kohr-DEH-roh ah-SAH-doh)
Roast lamb.

Empanada gallega (ehm-pah-NAH-dah gah-YEH-gah)
Chicken-filled bread pie.

Enchiladas rojas (ehn-chee-LAH-dahs RROH-hahs)
Corn tortillas dipped in spicy red sauce, fried, and stuffed with cheese, chicken, or meat.

Enchiladas verdes (ehn-chee-LAH-dahs BEHR-dehs)
Rolled corn tortillas stuffed with chicken or cheese and topped with green tomato sauce.

Feijoada (fey-SHWA-dah)
Feijoada could be considered the national dish of Brazil. There are many versions, but black beans and pork are the mainstays of this delicious meal. It is essentially a black bean stew with smoked and fresh pork, sometimes beef, sausages, onions, wine, oil, and spices. It is served with sliced oranges, wilted sliced kale, rice, and manioc flour. The drink of choice with *feijoada* is Brazilian rum.

Manchamanteles (mahn-cha-mahn-TEH-lehs)

Turkey, sausage, and chile stew seasoned with almonds, pineapple, apples, banana, and cinnamon. Literally means "tablecloth stainers."

Mole de guajolote (MOH-leh deh gwah-ho-LOH-te)

Turkey in chocolate, tomato, and nut sauce.

Mole is a Mexican specialty dating back to the seventeenth century. *Moles* of various types and colors can be found in most Mexican markets. They're essentially pastes of various chiles, nuts, chocolate, and spices used in the roasting and stewing of meats. Perhaps the most famous *mole* worldwide is the *mole poblano*. Go out of your way to try a *mole;* the flavors are bold and delicious.

Paella (pah-EH-yah)

Paella is one of the best-known Spanish dishes in the United States, and it certainly deserves its reputation as a delicious meal. Different versions crop up all over Latin America. Essentially, it consists of rice, often flavored with saffron, served with various meats, vegetables, and seafoods. The dish originated in Valencia, and *paella valenciana* is considered the ultimate even today. Earliest versions of *paella valenciana* included only snails and rabbit, but the version that is now world-famous has sausages, chicken, pork, clams, mussels, shrimp, and lobster. Combined with the highly flavored rice, this paella is truly delicious. It should be served with scallions to munch on, and order a nice, light red wine, maybe even a *sangría*.

Other *paella* variations are endless and, if properly prepared, can be outstanding. The biggest problem in American establishments is that many don't use the short-grain Spanish rice (long-grained rices don't hold up as well as the Spanish short-grained rice), and many cooks cover the *paella,* resulting in a steamy, overcooked product. The stripped-down version of *paella* is *arroz con pollo,* in which the rice is the same, but the only meat is chicken.

Picadillo (pee-kah-DEE-yoh)
Mexican hash.

Pipián (pee-PYAHN)
Pork meat in pumpkin-seed sauce.

Pollo a la chilindrón (POH-yoh AH LAH chee-leen-DROHN)
Sautéed chicken with peppers, tomatoes, and olives.

Puchero a la mexicana (poo-CHEH-roh ah lah meh-hee-KAH-nah)
Mexican boiled dinner, usually chicken or pork and vegetables in a soup.

Riñones al jerez (rree-NYOH-nehs AHL heh-rehs)
Sautéed kidneys with sherry sauce.

Ternera a la sevillana (tehr-NEH-rah AH LAH she-vee-YAH-nah)
Sautéed veal with sherry and green olives.

HOW DO YOU LIKE YOUR MEAT COOKED?

poco cocida/hecha	*rare*
POH-koh koh-SEE-dah/EH-chah	
en un término medio	*medium*
ehn oon TEHR-mee-noh MEH-dyoh	
bien cocida	*well done*
BYEHN koh-SEE-dah	

SEAFOOD ENTRÉES

Almejas a la marinera (ahl-MEH-hahs AH LAH mah-ree-NEH-rah)
   Clams cooked in white wine, garlic, tomatoes, and herbs.

Bacalao al ajo arriero (bah-kah-LAH-oh AHL AH-ho ahr-RYEH-roh)
   Salt cod with tomatoes, onion, and garlic.

Besugo al horno (beh-SOO-goh AHL OHR-noh)
   Red snapper baked with potatoes.

Calamares en su tinta (kah-lah-MAH-rehs EHN SOO TEEN-tah)
   Squid in their own ink.

Cazuela de Pescado (kah-SWEH-lah deh pehs-KAH-doh)
   Fish, potato, and rice casserole.

Ceviche acapulqueño (seh-VEE-cheh ah-kah-pool-KEH-nyoh)
   Raw fish or shellfish marinated in lime and orange juice and seasoned with tomato, onion, and hot pepper.

Guisado de pescado (gih-SAH-doh deh pehs-KAH-doh)

Fish and vegetable casserole.

Lenguado fino (lehn-GWAH-doh FEE-noh)

Dover sole.

> *Many restaurants have Dover sole on their menus, when in fact a different type of sole is being used. Dover sole, a king of fish in the culinary world, is only fished on the European side of the Atlantic Ocean. Its firm, succulent flesh makes it an incomparable eating fish, a very expensive fish, and a chef's favorite.*
>
> JIMMY TU, CHEF DE PARTIE,
> ELEVEN MADISON PARK, NEW YORK

Merluza a la gallega (mehr-LOO-sah AH LAH gah-YEH-gah)

Poached hake with potatoes and tomato sauce.

Peixada (pay-SHAH-dah)

Poached fish and shrimp, Brazilian style (with scallions, tomatoes, pepper, and coriander).

Vatapa (bah-tah-PAH)

Brazilian shrimp and coconut stew.

Zarzuela de mariscos (sahr-SWEH-lah deh mah-REES-kohs)

Catalonian shellfish stew.

Desserts and Sweets

Arequipe (ah-reh-KEE-peh)
Milk dessert made from cooking milk and sugar until it is very thick. Generally served with a guava jelly. Despite its richness, this is a very soothing dessert.

Arroz con leche (ah-RROHS COHN LEH-che)
Rice pudding. A true comfort food.

Ate (AH-teh)
Jellied paste made of different fruits, such as guava, apple, and quince.

Bizcocho borracho a la crema (bees-KOH-choh boh-RRAH-choh AH LAH KREH-mah)
Custard-filled, liqueur-flavored cake.

Brazo gitano (BRAH-soh he-TAH-noh)
Sponge-cake roll with rum cream filling.

Capirotada (kah-pee-roh-TAH-dah)
Bread pudding made with cheese, brown sugar, and dried fruits and various nuts in a cakelike form, usually eaten on Friday during Lent.

Chongos zamoranos (CHOHN-gohs sah-moh-RAH-nohs)
Egg yolks with milk and sugar, cooked with cinnamon and syrup.

Churros (CHOO-rrohs)
Crullers or doughnuts.

Flan (FLAHN)
Caramel custard. This is a dessert served in every Latin American country and Spain. Chances are the restaurant you visit will serve it as well.

Flan de naranja (FLAHN deh nah-RAHN-hah)
Orange caramel custard.

Leche frita (LEH-cheh FREE-tah)
Fried custard squares.

Natillas (nah-TEE-yahs)
Soft custard.

Pan de munición (PAHN deh moo-nee-SYOHN)
Chocolate custard cake.

Tarta de santiago (TAHR-tah deh sahn-TYAH-goh)
Almond cake.

Torta moca (TOHR-tah MOH-kah)
Mocha layer cake with rum.

Tortas de aceite (TOHR-tahs deh ah-SAY-teh)
Anise and sesame-seed cookies.

? DID YOU KNOW?

Chocolate comes from the cacao bean, whose name means "food of the gods." The Aztec emperor *Moctezuma* introduced the Spanish conquistadores to "xocolatl" in 1519. This was a beverage that, by law, only royalty could drink. Chocolate was so precious that the Maya and Aztec Indians used it as a form of currency. Chocolate was introduced to the European courts by Hernán Cortés and, by the mid-1600s, it had gained widespread popularity in France.

Wines and After-Dinner Drinks

WINES

SPAIN PRODUCES A GREAT DEAL of wine, much of it now exported. Spanish wines tend to be a bargain over better-known French and Italian wines, with some exceptions. *Riojas,* for example, from Spain's most prestigious wine area, are in much greater demand these days, and are priced accordingly. There is a full range of light- to heavy-bodied wines in both whites and reds. Ask your server for a suggestion, or, if you're in Spain, just have the local wine and savor it.

In South America, the two countries producing the most wine are Chile and Argentina. Both are relative newcomers on the international wine scene, and both produce some real bargains. Chardonnays, semillions, sauvignons, cabernets, and merlots are the most common grapes being used (all the most popular grapes in the United States today!). These wines are labeled by grape variety and vineyard, like American wines. Price will be your best guide for choosing the top examples.

AFTER-DINNER DRINKS

The first drink that comes to mind is sherry, Spain's most famous wine contribution to the world. While the dry sherries make excellent aperitifs, the heavier-bodied sweeter types are dessert wines. *Olorosos* and cream sherries are both excellent choices. Their sugar content makes them suitable not just for dessert, but for sipping in the evening while contemplating the great philosophers of the West, for example. Their modest alcohol content (when compared with brandies and other spirits) allows one more cerebral activity while partaking. What some people call "spoiled wine" others drink with relish.

Brandy

Spain has a relatively new (1987) brandy appellation, the third after Cognac and Armagnac in France. It is the *Denominación Específica* for *Brandy del Jerez*. The brandies from this region are unique in that they come from the same solera processing as sherry. Be sure to try one when you can. There are also many other brandies from Spain without the appellation. Spain is the largest domestic brandy consumer in Europe.

Kahlúa (kah-LOO-ah)

Mexico's grand contribution to the liqueur collection, a chocolate-coffee concoction. It's perhaps best when mixed with other ingredients. With coffee, it's marvelous, and with vodka as a "black Russian," it's marvelous *and* deadly.

Licor 43 (lee-KOHR kwah-REHN-tah E TREHS)

A yellow liqueur from Spain with vanilla and citrus flavors. Drink neat or on ice.

Pisco (PEES-koh)

Brandy from South America, lacking the finesse of fine world-caliber brandies, but packing the same punch. Some people enjoy *pisco* for its roughness, which sort of lets you know what you're drinking.

Rompope (rohm-POH-peh)

Rompope is very similar to egg nog, but spiked with rum.

Puebla, one of the most beautiful and religious colonial cities in Mexico, is famous for its contribution to Mexican cuisine. Mole, chiles ennogaola, and rompope— staples of traditional Mexican cuisine—were concocted here by Catholic nuns.

Coffee

COFFEE, *café* (kah-FEH), IS WIDELY CONSUMED throughout Spain and Latin America. Of course, some of the best coffee in the world is grown in Latin America and in the Caribbean. Colombian *supremo* is recognized as one of the top beans of the world, while Jamaican Blue Mountain is generally considered the absolute best.

Styles of coffee drinking vary from country to country, and even within countries. Espresso is seen in virtually all Latin countries and Spain, although the extreme dark roasting used in Italy is not universal. The Spaniards drink espresso with sugar and a small amount of cream, much like the Italian *macchiato*. Throughout South America it is common to drink a lighter roast at home and espresso in restaurants. Instant coffee is very common in South American homes because ground coffee is so expensive and frequently difficult to find because the lion's share of the crop is exported.

In general, you should simply order *café*, because there aren't different styles to choose from. You'll receive whatever *café* means in that particular restaurant. It's sure to be great, whatever the style!

CHECK, PLEASE!

La cuenta, por favor.	*The check, please.*
lah KWEHN-tah, pohr fah-VOHR.	
Hay un error.	*There's a mistake.*
ahy oon eh-ROHR.	
Todo estuvo muy bien.	*Everything was very good.*
TOH-doh ehs-TOO-voh MOOY BYEHN.	
Guarde el cambio.	*Keep the change.*
GWAHR-deh ehl KAHM-byoh.	

TIPPING

Tipping in Spain does not present a problem because a 10 to 15 percent service charge is added to most restaurant bills. However, many waiters expect a small tip on top. In Latin America most restaurants don't include a service charge, so make sure you tip the waiter at least 10 percent of the total bill. Feel free to tip 20 percent if you think the service is outstanding. Keep in mind that many of the waiters in Latin America earn less than $10 a day and that they really count on your tips (Americans and Canadians are known to be good tippers and usually receive excellent service).

Glossary of Ingredients and Techniques

Meats and Poultry

Albóndigas *(ahl-BOHN-dee-gahs)*
Meatballs.

Bistec *(bees-TEHK)*
Beef steak.

Cabrito *(kah-BREE-toh)*
Goat.

Callos *(KAH-yohs)*
Tripe.

Capone *(kah-POH-neh)*
Capon.

Carne *(KAHR-neh)*
Meat, either beef or veal. Used alone, it most often means beef. Technically, beef is *carne de vaca* or *carne de vacuno*, and veal is *carne de ternera*.

Carne fiambre *(KAHR-neh FYAHM-breh)*
Cold cuts.

Carne molida *(KAHR-neh moh-LEE-dah)*
Ground beef.

Carne picada *(KAHR-neh pee-KAH-dah)*
Chopped beef.

Carnero *(kahr-NEH-roh)*
Mutton.

Cecina *(seh-SEE-nah)*
Cured beef.

Cerdo *(SEHR-doh)*
Pork.

Chuleta de cordero *(choo-LEH-tah deh kohr-DEH-roh)*
Lamb chop.

Chuleta de ternera *(choo-LEH-tah deh tehr-NEH-rah)*
Veal chop.

Chuleto (choo-LEH-toh)
   Chop.

Churrasco (choo-RRAHS-koh)
   T-bone steak.

Cochinillo (koh-chee-NEE-yoh)
   Suckling pig.

Codornices (koh-door-NEE-sehs)
   Quail.

Conejo (koh-NEH-ho)
   Rabbit.

Corazón (koh-rah-SOHN)
   Heart.

Cordero (kohr-DEH-roh)
   Lamb.

Costilla (kohs-TEE-yah)
   Ribs.

Criadillas (kree-ha-DEE-yahs)
   Testicles.

Escalopines de ternera (ehs-kah-loh-PEE-nehs deh tehr-NEH-rah)
   Veal cutlets.

Faisán (fay-SAHN)
   Pheasant.

Ganso (GAHN-soh)
   Goose.

Guajolote (gwa-ho-LOH-teh)
   Turkey.

Hígado (EE-gah-doh)
   Calves' liver.

Jamón (hah-MOHN)
   Ham.

Lengua (LEHN-gwah)
   Tongue.

Lomo de cerdo *(LOH-moh deh SEHR-doh)*
  Pork loin.

Mollejas de ternera *(moh-YEH-has deh tehr-NEH-rah)*
  Veal sweetbreads (the thymus gland).

Oca *(OH-kah)*
  Goose.

Pato *(PAH-toh)*
  Duck.

Perdíz *(pehr-DEES)*
  Partridge.

Pollo *(POH-yoh)*
  Chicken.

Puerco *(PWER-koh)*
  Pork.

Rabo de toro *(RRAH-boh deh TOH-roh)*
  Oxtail.

Res *(REHS)*
  Beef.

Salchichón *(sahl-chee-CHOHN)*
  Thick salami.

Sesos *(SEH-sohs)*
  Brains.

Ternera *(tehr-NEH-rah)*
  Veal.

Venado *(beh-NAH-doh)*
  Venison.

Seafood

Almejas *(ahl-MEH-has)*
  Clams.

Anchoas *(ahn-CHOH-ahs)*
  Anchovies.

Anguilas *(ahn-GIH-lahs)*
  Eels.

Arenque *(ah-REHN-keh)*
Herring.

Atún *(ah-TOON)*
Tuna.

Bacalao *(bah-kah-LAH-oh)*
Salted codfish.

Calamares *(kah-lah-MAH-rehs)*
Squid.

Camarones *(kah-mah-ROH-nehs)*
Shrimp.

Cangrejos *(kahn-GREH-hos)*
Crabs.

Gambas *(GAHM-bahs)*
Shrimp/prawns.

Langosta *(lahn-GOH-stah)*
Lobster.

Langostinos *(lahn-gohs-TEE-nohs)*
Crayfish.

Ostras *(OHS-trahs)*
Oysters.

Pescado *(pehs-KAH-doh)*
Fish.

Pulpo *(POOL-poh)*
Octopus.

Sardinas *(sahr-DEE-nahs)*
Sardines.

Trucha *(TROO-chah)*
Trout.

Vegetables and Fruits

Aceituna *(ah-say-TOO-nah)*
Olive.

Albaricoque *(ahl-bah-ree-KOH-keh)*
Apricot.

Alcachofa (ahl-kah-CHOH-fah)
  Artichoke.

Apio (AH-pee-oh)
  Celery.

Berenjena (beh-rehn-HEH-nah)
  Eggplant.

Calabacín (kah-lah-bah-SEEN)
  Zucchini.

Calabaza (kah-lah-BAH-sah)
  Squash.

Cebolla (seh-BOH-yah)
  Onion.

Champiñon (chahm-pee-NYOHN)
  Mushroom.

Chícharo (CHEE-chah-roh)
  Pea.

Ciruela (see-RWEH-lah)
  Plum.

Coliflor (koh-lee-FLOOR)
  Cauliflower.

Durazno (doo-RAHS-noh)
  Peach.

Ejote (eh-HOH-teh)
  Green bean.

Elote (eh-LOH-teh)
  Corn.

Espárrago (ehs-PAH-rrah-goh)
  Asparagus.

Espinaca (ehs-pee-NAH-kah)
  Spinach.

Frambuesa (frahm-BWEH-sah)
  Raspberry.

Fresa (FREH-sah)
  Strawberry.

Frijoles (*free-*HOH*-lehs*)
Beans.

Guayaba (*gwah-*YAH*-bah*)
Guava.

Guisante (*gih-*SAHN*-teh*)
Pea.

Habas (*AH-bahs*)
Beans.

Higo (*EE-goh*)
Fig.

Tomate (*toh-*MAH*-teh*)
Tomato.

Judía (*hoo-*DEE*-ah*)
Green bean.

Lechuga (*leh-*CHOO*-gah*)
Lettuce.

Lentejas (*lehn-*TEH*-has*)
Lentils.

Lima (*LEE-mah*)
Key lime.

Limón (*lee-*MOHN*)
Lemon.

Maíz (*mah-*EES*)
Corn.

Mandarina (*mahn-dah-*REE*-nah*)
Tangerine.

Manioc (*mah-*NYOK*)
Also called the bitter cassava, a tuber. The plant is highly poisonous, containing hydrocyanic acid. Once this is removed, the tubers are ground into manioc flour, or *farinha de mandioca* (Portuguese). This is the single most important condiment in Brazil, and it's sprinkled on all sorts of foods. It is absolutely essential to *feijoada,* the national dish. See *yucca* for related sweet cassava.

Manzana (mahn-SAH-nah)
  Apple.

Melocotón (meh-loh-koh-TOHN)
  Peach.

Naranja (nah-RAHN-hah)
  Orange.

Papa (PAH-pah)
  Potato.

Pepino (peh-PEE-noh)
  Cucumber.

Pera (PEH-rah)
  Pear.

Pimiento (pee-MYEHN-toh)
  Bell pepper.

Piña (PEE-nyah)
  Pineapple.

Plátano (PLAH-tah-noh)
  Banana.

Puerro (PWEH-roh)
  Leek.

Repollo (reh-POH-yoh)
  Cabbage.

Sandía (sahn-DEE-ah)
  Watermelon.

Tapioca (tah-PYOH-kah)
  See *yucca*.

Tuna (TOO-nah)
  Prickly pear.

Uva (OO-vah)
  Grape.

Yucca (YOO-kah)
  The sweet cassava. This sweet cassava is often simply peeled, boiled, and then fried, and eaten as a starch. It is

also used extensively raw. Tapioca is made by processing the starch of the plant.

Zanahoria *(sah-nah-OH-ryah)*
Carrot.

Zapote *(sah-POH-teh)*
Sapodilla.

Herbs, Spices, and Condiments

Achiote *(ah-CHYOH-teh)*
Annatto.

Albahaca *(ahl-bah-AH-kah)*
Basil.

Alcaparra *(ahl-kah-PAH-rah)*
Caper.

Alcaravea *(ahl-kah-rah-VEH-ah)*
Caraway.

Anís *(ah-NEES)*
Anise.

Azafrán *(ah-sah-FRAIIN)*
Saffron.

Canela *(kah-NEH-lah)*
Cinnamon.

Cardamomo *(kahr-dah-MOH-moh)*
Cardamom.

Cebollino *(seh-boh-YEE-noh)*
Chive.

Cerafolio *(seh-rah-FOH-lyoh)*
Chervil.

Cilantro *(see-LAHN-troh)*
Cilantro, coriander leaves, or Chinese parsley.

Clavo *(KLAH-voh)*
Clove.

Comino *(koh-MEE-noh)*
Cumin.

Culantro (koo-LAHN-troh)
Cilantro, coriander.

Enebro (eh-NEH-broh)
Juniper.

Estragón (ehs-trah-GOHN)
Tarragon.

Hierbabuena (yehr-bah-BWEH-nah)
Mint.

Hinojo (ee-NOH-hoh)
Fennel.

Hoja de laurel (oh-ha deh lou-REHL)
Bay leaf.

Jengibre (hehn-HEE-breh)
Ginger.

Menta (MEHN-tah)
Mint.

*Nuez moscada
(NWEHS mohs-KAH-dah)*
Nutmeg.

Perejil (peh-reh-HEEL)
Parsley.

Pimentón (pee-mehn-TOHN)
Cayenne pepper.

Pimienta (blanca/negra) (pee-MYEHN-tah [BLAHN-kah/NEH-grah])
Pepper (white/black).

Pimienta húgara (pee-MYEHN-tah OO-gah-rah)
Paprika.

Pimienta inglesa (pee-MYEHN-tah een-GLEH-sah)
Allspice.

Romero (roh-MEH-roh)
Rosemary.

Salvia (SAHL-vyah)
Sage.

Tomillo (toh-MEE-yoh)
Thyme.

Dairy Products

Crema (KREH-mah)
Cream.

Huevos (WEH-vohs)
Eggs.

Leche (LEH-cheh)
Milk.

Mantequilla (mahn-teh-KEE-yah)
Butter.

Nata (NAH-tah)
Cream.

Queso (KEH-soh)
Cheese.

Suggested Menus

—∞—

A Tapas Menu for Relaxing with Friends

The drink of choice for this meal is sangría.

Almendras saladas
Salted almonds

Aceitunas aliñadas
Marinated olives

Pepinillos en vinagre
Gherkins in vinegar

Caracoles de Borgoña
Snails with butter, garlic, and parsley

Buñuelos de queso
Cheese fritters

Albóndigas
Pork meatballs

A Hearty Fall Dinner

Aperitif: Lightly chilled fino sherry

Empanada de espinacas
Spinach turnovers

(Dry white wine, also to be served with the soup)

Sopa de pescado y almendras
Fish and almond soup

Carne de puerco en adobo
Pork loin in aciote and chile sauce

(full-bodied red wine, such as a Rioja; or try a semi-dry white, such as a Rioja blanca)

Flan de naranja
Orange flan (custard)

Jerez
Sherry

Café
Coffee

Simple but Elegant Supper Menu

Sopa de aguacate
Avocado soup

Paella valenciana
Valencian-style paella (saffron rice with meats and seafoods)

(full-bodied dry white wine, such as a Monopole from Rioja)

Tarta de Santiago
Almond cake

Mexican Fantasy Menu

Aperitif: Margaritas en las rocas

Sopa de tortilla
Soup with fried tortilla strips, avocado, fresh cream,
and beef brains

(Mexican beer, to be drunk throughout meal)

Mole poblano
Turkey or chicken braised in a roasted chile sauce with
a bit of chocolate added. Serve with flour or corn
tortillas.

Arroz con leche
Rice pudding.

Café
Coffee

Brazilian Bash Menu

Serve a *batida brasileira* with this meal, which is a
sour made from the native *cachaça*, a type of rum.

Feijoada
Black beans with various pork cuts, both fresh and
smoked, plus sausage. Served with orange segments,
rice, and kale. Manioc powder is sprinkled over everything.

Peras assadas
Baked pears

TIPPING CHART

TOTAL	15%	20%	TOTAL	15%	20%
$5	0.75	$1.00	$29	$4.35	$5.80
$6	$0.90	$1.20	$30	$4.50	$6.00
$7	$1.05	$1.40	$31	$4.65	$6.20
$8	$1.20	$1.60	$32	$4.80	$6.40
$9	$1.35	$1.80	$33	$4.95	$6.60
$10	$1.50	$2.00	$34	$5.10	$6.80
$11	$1.65	$2.20	$35	$5.25	$7.00
$12	$1.80	$2.40	$36	$5.40	$7.20
$13	$1.95	$2.60	$37	$5.55	$7.40
$14	$2.10	$2.80	$38	$5.70	$7.60
$15	$2.25	$3.00	$39	$5.85	$7.80
$16	$2.40	$3.20	$40	$6.00	$8.00
$17	$2.55	$3.40	$41	$6.15	$8.20
$18	$2.70	$3.60	$42	$6.30	$8.40
$19	$2.85	$3.80	$43	$6.45	$8.60
$20	$3.00	$4.00	$44	$6.60	$8.80
$21	$3.15	$4.20	$45	$6.75	$9.00
$22	$3.30	$4.40	$46	$6.90	$9.20
$23	$3.45	$4.60	$47	$7.05	$9.40
$24	$3.60	$4.80	$48	$7.20	$9.60
$25	$3.75	$5.00	$49	$7.35	$9.80
$26	$3.90	$5.20	$50	$7.50	$10.00
$27	$4.05	$5.40	$51	$7.65	$10.20
$28	$4.20	$5.60	$52	$7.80	$10.40

TIPPING CHART

TOTAL	15%	20%	TOTAL	15%	20%
$53	$7.95	$10.60	$77	$11.55	$15.40
$54	$8.10	$10.80	$78	$11.70	$15.60
$55	$8.25	$11.00	$79	$11.85	$15.80
$56	$8.40	$11.20	$80	$12.00	$16.00
$57	$8.55	$11.40	$81	$12.15	$16.20
$58	$8.70	$11.60	$82	$12.30	$16.40
$59	$8.85	$11.80	$83	$12.45	$16.60
$60	$9.00	$12.00	$84	$12.60	$16.80
$61	$9.15	$12.20	$85	$12.75	$17.00
$62	$9.30	$12.40	$86	$12.90	$17.20
$63	$9.45	$12.60	$87	$13.05	$17.40
$64	$9.60	$12.80	$88	$13.20	$17.60
$65	$9.75	$13.00	$89	$13.35	$17.80
$66	$9.90	$13.20	$90	$13.50	$18.00
$67	$10.05	$13.40	$91	$13.65	$18.20
$68	$10.20	$13.60	$92	$13.80	$18.40
$69	$10.35	$13.80	$93	$13.95	$18.60
$70	$10.50	$14.00	$94	$14.10	$18.80
$71	$10.65	$14.20	$95	$14.25	$19.00
$72	$10.80	$14.40	$96	$14.40	$19.20
$73	$10.95	$14.60	$97	$14.55	$19.40
$74	$11.10	$14.80	$98	$14.70	$19.60
$75	$11.25	$15.00	$99	$14.85	$19.80
$76	$11.40	$15.20	$100	$15.00	$20.00

TIPPING CHART

TOTAL	15%	20%	TOTAL	15%	20%
$101	$15.15	$20.20	$126	$18.90	$25.20
$102	$15.30	$20.40	$127	$19.05	$25.40
$103	$15.45	$20.60	$128	$19.20	$25.60
$104	$15.60	$20.80	$129	$19.35	$25.80
$105	$15.75	$21.00	$130	$19.50	$26.00
$106	$15.90	$21.20	$131	$19.65	$26.20
$107	$16.05	$21.40	$132	$19.80	$26.40
$108	$16.20	$21.60	$133	$19.95	$26.60
$109	$16.35	$21.80	$134	$20.10	$26.80
$110	$16.50	$22.00	$135	$20.25	$27.00
$111	$16.65	$22.20	$136	$20.40	$27.20
$112	$16.80	$22.40	$137	$20.55	$27.40
$113	$16.95	$22.60	$138	$20.70	$27.60
$114	$17.10	$22.80	$139	$20.85	$27.80
$115	$17.25	$23.00	$140	$21.00	$28.00
$116	$17.40	$23.20	$141	$21.15	$28.20
$117	$17.55	$23.40	$142	$21.30	$28.40
$118	$17.70	$23.60	$143	$21.45	$28.60
$119	$17.85	$23.80	$144	$21.60	$28.80
$120	$18.00	$24.00	$145	$21.75	$29.00
$121	$18.15	$24.20	$146	$21.90	$29.20
$122	$18.30	$24.40	$147	$22.05	$29.40
$123	$18.45	$24.60	$148	$22.20	$29.60
$124	$18.60	$24.80	$149	$22.35	$29.80
$125	$18.75	$25.00	$150	$22.50	$30.00

TOTAL	15%	20%	TOTAL	15%	20%
$151	$22.65	$30.20	$176	$26.40	$35.20
$152	$22.80	$30.40	$177	$26.55	$35.40
$153	$22.95	$30.60	$178	$26.70	$35.60
$154	$23.10	$30.80	$179	$26.85	$35.80
$155	$23.25	$31.00	$180	$27.00	$36.00
$156	$23.40	$31.20	$181	$27.15	$36.20
$157	$23.55	$31.40	$182	$27.30	$36.40
$158	$23.70	$31.60	$183	$27.45	$36.60
$159	$23.85	$31.80	$184	$27.60	$36.80
$160	$24.00	$32.00	$185	$27.75	$37.00
$161	$24.15	$32.20	$186	$27.90	$37.20
$162	$24.30	$32.40	$187	$28.05	$37.40
$163	$24.45	$32.60	$188	$28.20	$37.60
$164	$24.60	$32.80	$189	$28.35	$37.80
$165	$24.75	$33.00	$190	$28.50	$38.00
$166	$24.90	$33.20	$191	$28.65	$38.20
$167	$25.05	$33.40	$192	$28.80	$38.40
$168	$25.20	$33.60	$193	$28.95	$38.60
$169	$25.35	$33.80	$194	$29.10	$38.80
$170	$25.50	$34.00	$195	$29.25	$39.00
$171	$25.65	$34.20	$196	$29.40	$39.20
$172	$25.80	$34.40	$197	$29.55	$39.40
$173	$25.95	$34.60	$198	$29.70	$39.60
$174	$26.10	$34.80	$199	$29.85	$39.80
$175	$26.25	$35.00	$200	$30.00	$40.00

ABOUT THE AUTHOR

DAVID D'APRIX began his cooking career at the age of seven, when he prepared his first batch of oatmeal. Fifteen years later, after completing a Bachelor of Arts degree in liberal arts, D'Aprix remembered the thrill of making that porridge. He enrolled in the Culinary Institute of America and graduated in 1977. In addition to extensive experience in the hotel and restaurant industries, D'Aprix has been on the faculty in the School of Hotel Administration at Cornell University, where he currently lectures, and has given seminars in many countries throughout the world. He lives in Ithaca, New York, with his wife and two children.